ONE REAL AMERICAN

ONE REAL AMERICAN

The Life of Ely S. Parker

SENECA SACHEM AND CIVIL WAR GENERAL

JOSEPH BRUCHAC

ABRAMS BOOKS FOR YOUNG READERS ★ NEW YORK

DEDICATED TO MY MANY FRIENDS AMONG
THE SIX NATIONS,
WITH SINCERE THANKS FOR ALL OF THEIR HELP
AND GUIDANCE OVER THE PAST HALF CENTURY

The inspiration for the border design and other motifs comes from the
beadwork and basket weaving collections at the Seneca Iroquois National Museum
and Fenimore Art Museum as well as Iroquoisbeadwork.blogspot.com.

Cataloging-in-Publication Data has been applied for
and may be obtained from the Library of Congress.

ISBN 978-1-4197-4657-4

Text copyright © 2020 Joseph Bruchac
Edited by Howard W. Reeves
Book design by Sara Corbett

Printed and bound in U.S.A.
10 9 8 7 6 5 4 3 2 1

Abrams Books for Young Readers are available at special discounts when
purchased in quantity for premiums and promotions as well as fundraising
or educational use. Special editions can also be created to specification.
For details, contact specialsales@abramsbooks.com or the address below.

ABRAMS The Art of Books
195 Broadway, New York, NY 10007
abramsbooks.com

CONTENTS

Note: The Six Nations of the Haudenosaunee, the People of the Long-house, have been known by different names since the coming of Europeans. Although they did not originally use those names themselves, such names as "Iroquois" for the Haudenosaunee, the People of the Longhouse, and "Seneca" for the Onondowaga, the Great Hill People, have become so familiar and commonly used that contemporary Haudenosaunee people are comfortable with those names and use them on a daily basis. They appear in the historic record of federal and government relations with the Senecas and Iroquois as a whole. Ely S. Parker in his writings and everyday life referred to himself as Seneca and to the Six Nations as the League of the Iroquois. It is for those reasons that I've chosen to use "Iroquois" and "Seneca" throughout this book.

Some Iroquois names in this book are hyphenated, and some are not (and some are written both ways), which reflects the way that Iroquois words were written in English in different time periods and by different writers.

A MEETING AT APPOMATTOX

I was present at the meeting of the two generals commanding the two great contending armies, Grant and Lee, the one quiet, modest and reticent, the other dignified, but broken. I saw the one write his terms for surrender, and the other his acceptance of the same. I hold in my hand an original of General Grant's terms of surrender in his own handwriting, and which I, as military secretary, transferred into ink before it was passed to Lee.

—FROM GENERAL ELY S. PARKER'S AUTOBIOGRAPHY

April 9, 1865, was a warm spring Sunday in the town of Appomattox Court House, Virginia. Accompanied by several members of his staff, General Ulysses S. Grant approached the house of Wilmer McLean, who had offered the use of his parlor for the signing of General Robert E. Lee's terms of surrender of the Army of Northern Virginia. It was an event, in that modest two-story building, that would mark the formal conclusion of hostilities between the North and South, although there were other battles lasting until the Cherokee Confederate General Stand Watie gave up in June of that year. It would bring an end to the American Civil War, one of the most brutal struggles in the history of the United States.

MCLEAN HOUSE AT APPOMATTOX COURT HOUSE, VIRGINIA

Inside that house, dressed in a new full uniform and wearing the ceremonial sword given to him by his beloved home state of Virginia, Robert E. Lee, the brilliant southern commander, waited.

A MEETING AT APPOMATTOX

That uniform, as Grant himself would later note in his memoirs, was a contrast to what the leader of the Union forces appeared in.

"In my rough traveling suit, the uniform of a private with the straps of a lieutenant-general, I must have contrasted very strangely with a man so handsomely dressed, six feet high and of faultless form. But this was not a matter that I thought of until afterwards."

Lee's retreat after Petersburg and Richmond fell into Union hands had been blocked by Grant. The charismatic southern leader's only choice, one he found hard to make, had been to accept defeat. He'd sent a note to Grant asking for an interview to discuss terms of surrender.

That note, as Grant's personal secretary Brevet Brigadier General Ely S. Parker would later recall, was read by Grant with no outward show of emotion. That was no surprise, for Grant was famously taciturn. Grant's staff, however, reacted quite differently.

As Parker put it, "The Staff had a little jollification of their own on the lonely road in the woods by cheering, throwing up their hats, and performing such other antics as their tired limbs and dignity would permit."

Grant's reply to Lee, written by Parker, who was always by his side, indicated his readiness to meet. It was delivered by one of Grant's aides, General Orville Elias Babcock, who now stood waiting for Grant in front of the house's wide front porch. While he ushered the Union's commanding general up the steps and into the parlor, the rest of Grant's staff sat down on the porch. But only for a moment. Babcock soon returned to the door.

"The General wants you all to come in," he said.

What happened next, the formal introduction by Grant of each of his staff members to General Lee, went smoothly at first. As Parker noted, Lee "shook hands with each in the most courteous, condescending and yet affable manner, making no remark further than passing the usual salutation."

Until Parker himself held out his own hand. According to Lieutenant Colonel Horace Porter, another of Grant's secretaries, "When Lee saw his swarthy features he looked at him in evident surprise, and his eyes rested on him for several seconds. What was passing in his mind, no one knew, but the natural surmise was that he at first mistook Parker for a negro, and was struck with astonishment to find the commander of Union armies had one of that race on his personal staff."

Whatever General Robert E. Lee had been thinking, he soon recognized that the dark skin of the person before him, though dressed in a Union uniform, marked him not as one of African ancestry, but as a Native American.

"I am glad to see one real American here," Lee said as he took Ely Parker's hand.

"We are all Americans," Parker replied.

As the meeting progressed, Parker continued to play a very visible role. Colonel Theodore S. Bowers, one of Grant's adjutant generals, had brought the papers for the surrender. Bowers, a former newspaper editor, had enlisted as a private and rose rapidly through the ranks to become one of Grant's favorites. That day, though, awed by the occasion, he was visibly nervous. Parker helped him arrange the papers as Grant sat smoking his pipe.

When Grant indicated he was ready, it was Parker who handed him the manifold order book. In those days, a manifold order book, several bound sheets of thin yellow paper with carbon inserts, was used to produce duplicate copies. Grant wrote out his terms and passed them over the table to Lee. A few changes were agreed upon and Parker wrote them in the book.

The manifold book was then returned to Bowers for him to make the official copy in ink. He tried to do so, but his hands were shaking and he destroyed one sheet after another. Finally he gave up the task.

"Parker," he said, "you will have to write this. I can't do it."

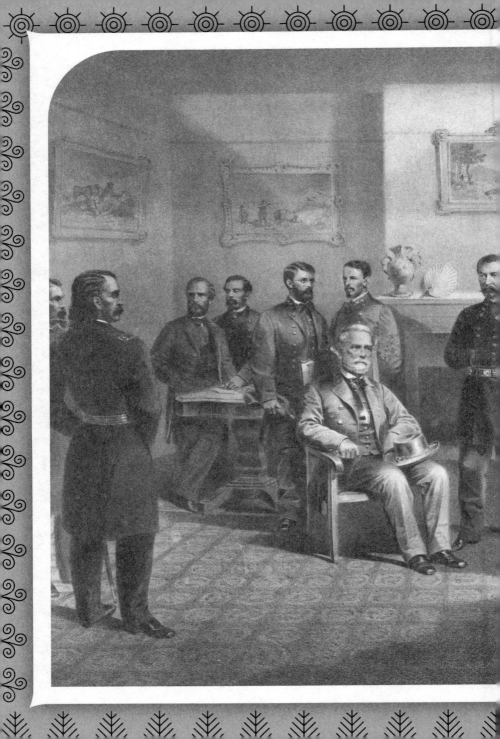

PRINT OF THE ROOM IN THE MCLEAN HOUSE IN WHICH GEN. ROBERT E. LEE SURRENDERED TO GEN. ULYSSES S. GRANT ON APRIL 9, 1865. ELY PARKER IS STANDING, THIRD FROM RIGHT.

ONE REAL AMERICAN

So it was that the official terms of surrender marking the end of the Civil War were written in the hand of Ely S. Parker. Ely S. Parker, who was not only the highest ranking Native American in the Union Army but also bore the title of Donehogawa (the Guardian of the Western door) as a Seneca Grand Sachem of the Haudenosaunee—the League of the Iroquois.

2

WHO ARE THE IROQUOIS?

The ancient League is legitimately entitled to great praise and honor among the expiring peoples of the earth . . . In their simplicity they early discovered, adopted and exemplified the incontrovertible and wise political doctrine, that in union there is strength.

—ELY S. PARKER, FROM A LETTER DATED JULY 22, 1887

There was a time when the Haudenosaunee, the five Native nations commonly known as the Iroquois, were constantly at war with one another. Those five nations, who spoke different dialects of the same language, were the Mohawks, the Oneidas, the Onondagas, the Cayugas, and the Senecas. They lived in great longhouses covered with elm bark in stockaded villages. They viewed their confederacy as being shaped like one of those

Scenes About a —
Seneca Bark
Lodge —

J. J. Cornplanter
1905

SCENE FROM AN IROQUOIS BARK LONGHOUSE BY JESSE CORNPLANTER, 1905

traditional structures. Although those large longhouses sometimes sheltered hundreds of people in family apartments on either side of the central fires, that symbolic longhouse of the Great League was even more immense. It stretched across what is now New York State from the Hudson River in the east to the Niagara River in the west. The Mohawks in the east were the guardians of the eastern door, through the traditional entrance of a physical longhouse. The Onondagas kept the fire in the center in the area of present-day Syracuse. The Senecas, as the westernmost of the original Five Nations, had the job of guarding that door, beyond which were

MAP OF THE IROQUOIS FIVE NATIONS AS IT WAS AROUND 1650. TONAWANDA RESERVATION, ESTABLISHED CIRCA 1750, THE BIRTHPLACE OF ELY PARKER, IS ALSO SHOWN.

all of the western tribes that were sometimes at odds with the Confederacy.

Once, they had lived together in peace, but that time had passed. All of their oral traditions speak eloquently of that bitter age of raid and counterraid, constant revenge and brutal retribution. No one was safe, not even the women and children or elders. As Jake Swamp, a subchief of the Mohawk Nation explained it, "We were the worst people in the world back then."

That is when, perhaps a thousand years ago, a miracle happened. A boy was born among the Wendat people who lived to the west, on the shores of Lake Ontario, On-ia-de-lee-yoh, the Beautiful Lake. As soon as he could speak, his every word was of peace. He bore a name that is regarded so sacred it is only spoken in ceremony, so he became known as the Peacemaker. When he was old enough, he made a canoe of stone and sailed across the lake to the lands of those five warring nations. His mission was to unite them in peace.

Among the Iroquois nations, the women have always played a central role, heading the households and caring for the land.

A DUPLICATE OF THE ORIGINAL CENTURIES-OLD FIVE NATIONS OF HIAWATHA WAMPUM BELT. IT SYMBOLIZES THE FOUNDING OF THE IROQUOIS CONFEDERACY. EACH SQUARE REPRESENTS AN IROQUOIS NATION. ON THE FAR LEFT IS THE SENECA NATION; ON THE FAR RIGHT IS THE MOHAWK NATION; AND THE ONEIDA AND CAYUGA NATIONS ARE IN BETWEEN. THE CENTRAL TREE IS THE ONONDAGA NATION. (THE TUSCARORA NATION JOINED THE IROQUOIS CONFEDERACY IN THE EARLY 1700S SO IS NOT REPRESENTED IN THIS EARLY BELT.)

To this day, a person's clan is inherited from the mother and each of the several clans in each nation is headed by a clan mother. So, it is significant that one of the Peacemaker's first disciples was Jigonsaseh, an influential woman who embraced and endorsed his idea of bringing peace.

Aided by an eloquent Mohawk leader named Hiawatha, who was the second to enlist in his cause, the Peacemaker went to one Haudenosaunee nation after another. Though it was no easy task, his words and his deeds convinced those nations, one by one, to lay down their weapons and join what became known as the Great Peace.

The last to agree to the Great Peace were the Onondagas. Led by Tadadaho, a powerful chief—described as an evil sorcerer in all Iroquois traditions—they refused to hear the Peacemaker's words. Tadadaho was a giant of a man with snakes—evidence of his twisted mind—growing from his hair, and seven crooks in his body. Whenever the Peacemaker and his disciples tried to approach him, he would use his magic to escape. It was not until all his people joined their voice in a hymn of peace, that Tadadaho became so entranced that he could not move. The Peacemaker and Hiawatha then straightened his body while Hiawatha—whose name means "the Comber"—combed the snakes from the giant chief's hair.

His mind no longer twisted, Tadadaho was set up as the head of the council of fifty royaners, representatives chosen by the clan mothers of each nation, to govern the united peoples. A war club was symbolically planted beneath a pine tree that represented the new league. An eagle holding five arrows in its talons was placed atop the tree, which had white roots stretching to the four directions, East, South, West, and North. Those five arrows, easy to break one by one, but strong when bound together, stood for the five nations now governed as one.

To this day, the names of those fifty original representatives are passed down from one leader to the next, still chosen by the clan mothers. Thus, there is always a Tadadaho at Onondaga.

That powerful League of the Iroquois became known as the Six Nations after the Tuscaroras joined them in 1722.

When the Europeans came, the League of the Iroquois found itself in a unique position, both geographically and politically. As the strongest and most united of the northeastern tribal nations, they were valued as military allies during the decades-long struggle for North America between France and England in the first half of the eighteenth century. The territory the Iroquois controlled, roughly from the Hudson River in the east to Lake Ontario in the west, was the major corridor—along the Mohawk River—for western

Nations grew tired of dealing with the different rules for trade they encountered with each of the separate northeastern colonies. Benjamin Franklin and others were invited to meetings of the Iroquois League to observe how a central government and common rules would be beneficial.

When the American Revolution began, both the British and the breakaway colonies sought the Iroquois as an ally. At the start of the American Revolution, a meeting of the League was held to decide which side they would align themselves with—the Crown or the Colonies. However, they could not all agree on which to support. Because consensus and total unanimity was required for the League to make a decision, in the end the council fire that was lit whenever the members of the League met was ceremonially covered. Each of the Six Nations was free to make its own choice.

The Oneidas supported the thirteen colonies and served—quite effectively—on their side. If it were not for the hundreds of bushels of corn and other food brought by a faction of the Oneidas to General George Washington when his winter-bound troops were in danger of starving at Valley Forge, the Revolution might have failed. Most of the Iroquois fighters, though, including Joseph Brant's Mohawks, joined the English side.

The Iroquois did not fare well in the American Revolution. The surrender of the British—who ceded their colonial lands and generally abandoned their Native allies—left them vulnerable. The most devastating blow was felt by the Senecas, the victims of the 1779 Sullivan Expedition, a scorched-earth raid of Iroquois lands meant to bring the war home to the enemy to break their morale. Lasting from June through September, more than forty Iroquois villages were destroyed along with millions of bushels of corn, their winter stores. After the war, the controversial Treaty of Fort Stanwix (signed under duress and later rejected by the Iroquois Confederacy) greatly reduced the formerly vast land base of the Iroquois nations. In that treaty the Six Nations also pledged to never again make war against the new American nation and to always be its ally.

The tragic results of the Revolution for the Iroquois were threefold. First, for the only time since the founding of the league, Iroquois people had found themselves sometimes fighting other Iroquois. Second, the war devastated large parts of the Iroquois homeland. Third, after the war, the Iroquois who remained in the United States found themselves confined to tiny parts of their formerly vast territories on those small reservations in western, central, and far-northern New York. They were also now divided between Canada and the United States.

Some Mohawks followed Joseph Brant to that new reserve in Ontario provided by his British allies. Other Mohawks relocated on four reserves in Quebec, Gibson, Kahnawake, and Kanesatake and the St. Regis Reservation (now known as Akwesasne) that is partially in Canada and partially in the United States on the St. Lawrence River. The Onondagas kept a four-mile-by-four-mile reservation in the heart of their original territory. Many of the Oneidas went to Wisconsin, with only a few families remaining on a forty-acre plot of land in their central New York homeland. The Tuscaroras kept a reservation near Niagara Falls, while the Cayugas ended up as refugees at Six Nations territory in Ontario and on Cattaraugus Seneca lands with no New York land base at all. The Senecas, formerly the most numerous and powerful of Iroquois nations, found themselves, after the 1784 treaty, confined to several small pieces of land in western New York.

The last decades of the eighteenth century were, not surprisingly, a time of great turmoil and distress for the Iroquois. Alcoholism became common and many white observers felt that the Iroquois would melt away like the snow in spring. But they were more resilient than European Americans thought and survived that difficult time. One factor in their survival was the arrival of a new spiritual tradition that was accepted by many in all the Six Nations. A Seneca man who bore the chieftaincy name of Ganio'dai'io', or Handsome Lake, had a visionary experience. He awoke from a near-death coma brought on by drinking to relate a series of prophetic visions given to him by Four Messengers from Ha-wen-ne'-yu, the Creator. The half brother of Cornplanter, a deeply respected Seneca leader, Handsome Lake's words proved to be enormously influential. His experience led to the establishment of a new way—the Gai'wiio, or Good Message, emphasized morality, peace, family ties, and sobriety and might have been influenced by Quaker practices. It so impressed Thomas Jefferson that the president had his secretary of war, Henry Dearborn, write a letter commending the prophet, which was delivered to a Seneca delegation visiting Washington, D.C.:

> Brothers—The President is pleased with seeing you all in good health, after so long a journey, and he rejoices in his heart that one of your own people has employed to make you sober, good and happy; and that he is so well disposed to give you good advice, and to set before you so good examples.

> Brothers—If all the red people follow the example of your friend and teacher, the Handsome Lake, and in future will be sober, honest, industrious and good, there can be no doubt but the Great Spirit will take care of you and make you happy.

Dearborn's letter certainly added to Handsome Lake's prestige among the Iroquois, many seeing it as something like a license for him to preach. Others, however, such as Red Jacket, an influential Seneca elder and famous orator, viewed him as a charlatan and bitterly opposed his teachings.

Over the next sixteen years, from 1799 until his death in 1815, Handsome Lake refined, added to, and taught his precepts among the Six Nations. Handsome Lake's teachings, which became known as the Longhouse Religion, were not universally accepted and he was driven from his home on the Allegany Reservation. However, he found refuge on the Tonawanda Seneca Reservation, 180 miles to the north. There his successor, Chief Jemmy Johnson, or Sose-ha-wa, who was the prophet's nephew (but called his grandson), continued his teachings. Tonawanda became the center of both the new religion and resistance to further removal of the Senecas from their lands.

The new Longhouse Religion—which also strongly condemned the sale of Indian land—was one of the factors that led to the survival, against all odds, of the Tonawanda Reservation. There was also a recognition among the elders of all six nations that they would have to find a way to work with the American nation that now surrounded them on all sides. One of their strategies was to choose promising young Iroquois men to be sent from their communities to learn the ways of the white man. By gaining a European-style education, such men could then act as defenders of their people's interests—especially in protecting what little land was left to them from white men seeking to take it. They could, in the old tradition of men being chosen to carry wampum-belt messages from one nation to another, become "runners." Their destinations would not be other Indian communities, however, but the white centers of power in Albany and Washington.

Going to Washington to defend their interests was not a new thing for the Senecas. Despite the fact that he had been forced to put his name on a treaty in 1826, Red Jacket was known for strongly opposing the sale of Indian lands.

Red Jacket's Seneca name, Sagoyewatha (He Who Keeps Them Awake), reflected his legendary abilities as an orator. He was the most famous Indian of his time, well known to the white world for his speeches, which were often translated into English and published in newspapers.

Even though he only spoke in Seneca, white people would come to listen to him because of the beauty and power of his voice. It was said that he had gained his oratorical strength by standing close to the cataract of Niagara Falls and absorbing its roaring power. To this day, a statue of Red Jacket stands next to the falls.

SAGOYEWATHA. RED JACKET WEARING PEACE MEDAL, PAINTING (DETAIL) BY CHARLES BIRD KING.

One story about Red Jacket tells of how he took a walk along the Niagara River with a man who called himself a friend of the Indians. Red Jacket sat down with him on a log near the river. Then Red Jacket shifted closer to the man.

"Move over," Red Jacket said.

The man moved, only to have Red Jacket slide up to him and say, "Move over" a second time.

This went on until the white man was at the very end of the log.

"Move over," Red Jacket said yet again.

"But if I move further, I shall fall into the water," the man protested.

Red Jacket nodded. "And even so, you white people tell us to move on when there is no place left to go."

Handsome Lake, in one of his later visions, saw his enemy Red Jacket doomed to carry burdens of soil for eternity as punishment for his role in signing that Buffalo Creek Treaty of 1826. A deceptive agreement forced on the Senecas, it ceded the entire Buffalo Creek Reservation—land that became the city of Buffalo—to a development group called the Ogden Land Company.

Red Jacket led Seneca delegations to Albany and to Washington, where he spoke directly with President John Quincy Adams. That the 1826 treaty was never ratified by Congress was in part because of Red Jacket's appeal to allow the Senecas to hold on to what little land remained theirs. However, the fact remained that a treaty ceding the Seneca land existed and those lands were highly desirable.

By 1826, due to earlier cessions, the Ogden Land Company had already gained access to millions of acres formerly owned by the Senecas. But the greed of the Ogden Company was not satisfied. They did everything in their power, including bribery and the use of force, to dispossess the remaining Indians—who they publicly described as ignorant, uncivilized, and savage.

The Senecas, however, were far from uncivilized or ignorant. Although few were fluent in English, they had been trading with Europeans for generations. The Tonawanda clan mothers, and the men these women chose to represent their nation, had a much better understanding of the white world surrounding them than the vast majority of white people had of the Native American world.

An example of that sophisticated Seneca understanding of the new world in which they lived came in 1812. The new American nation faced a threat from an old enemy. At the start of the War of 1812, the second armed conflict with England, many Americans feared the Senecas would aid their former British allies. In fact, the colonies of Upper and Lower Canada were saved, in large part, from American attachment by the wholesale participation of the Canadian Mohawks in alliance with the British and Canadians. Although Handsome Lake spoke against taking part in a "white man's war," the Seneca leaders decided otherwise. In a decision that was both strategic and patriotic, the Seneca nation declared its support for the American cause. Not only would they state their loyalty, they would risk their lives to prove it. They would fulfill their treaty obligation to always support the United States—and also engage in one of the most honored of pursuits for young men, defending their homeland—winning the respect of their white neighbors in the process.

Tonawandas joined the American army in proportionately large numbers. They engaged in many of the crucial battles of the western frontier as soldiers and scouts. More than ninety men, half the adult male population of Tonawanda, enlisted. Among their number was Red Jacket and a stocky eighteen-year-old Seneca warrior named Jo-no-es-sto-wa, or Dragonfly, whose European name was William Parker. He and his two brothers, Samuel and Henry, had taken the last name of Parker from an Englishman who had been adopted by the Senecas. For his two years of service during the war, in which he was wounded, William Parker received an army pension. And it is to that determined young man and his remarkable family that this story now turns.

OF NOBLE
BIRTH

That the General is an Indian you can each see for yourself.
Some fifty years ago he was born of poor, but honest
Indian parents in Genesee County, in the western part of
the State of New York. Indians are always poor, though
not always honest. Such a thing as a rich North American
Indian I do not think was ever known. Those parents I have
spoken of were members of the Seneca Nation of Indians,
one of the group of Indians who comprised the famous Five
Nations or Confederacy of Iroquois Indians of New York.

—FROM GENERAL ELY S. PARKER'S AUTOBIOGRAPHY

Following the War of 1812, during which he was seriously
wounded in the battle for Fort Niagara and later received a
pension for his injury, William Parker established himself as
a farmer on the small Tonawanda Reservation—its twenty fertile
square miles one of the few tracts of land remaining in Iroquois
hands after the Revolution. He did well—not only in farming but
also operating a sawmill along Tonawanda Creek. He was well

JO-NO-ES-STO-WA.
WILLIAM PARKER.

respected, as was his brother Samuel, who had already become a chief. William's generosity and hospitality were both typically Seneca and legendary—always ready to help a neighbor, his door open to anyone who traveled by, including Red Jacket, who was a frequent visitor and the great-uncle of William's wife.

Not long after his return from the war, William married. Since he had become a convert to Christianity, he and his bride were married by Abel Bingham, the Baptist missionary who had established a small church on the reservation.

William's wife, Ga-ont-gwut-twus, or Wolf Woman, was seven years older—typical of Iroquois marriages at that time. And he married well—very well, indeed. Ga-ont-gwut-twus was even more respected in the Seneca community than her husband. Born in 1786, she bore the English name Elizabeth Johnson and was the niece of Chief Jemmy Johnson, Sose-ha-wa, the successor of Handsome Lake.

In addition to those outstanding paternal roots, Elizabeth

Parker's maternal ancestry traced back to Jigonsaseh, the first woman to embrace the ideas of the Peacemaker. She was one of prestigious birth.

Her maternal ancestry made her a member of the Wolf Clan. In the Iroquois way, clan is always passed down from mother to child, making that part of a person's heritage much more import-

GA-ONT-GWUT-TWUS.
ELIZABETH PARKER.

ant than that of the father's. When an Iroquois man becomes a royaner, one of the fifty representatives of his people in the Great League, it is only through being selected by the women of his clan.

It is sometimes difficult for non-Natives to understand the importance of clan among the Iroquois. The Senecas have a total of eight clans, groups of families each bearing the name of the bird or animal that provided special help to the people in the past. Your clan may even show itself in one's personality. A member of the Turtle Clan, for example, might be more measured and deliberate, while one of the Wolf Clan might be more outwardly demonstrative and quicker moving. Those in a particular clan—even if from a different tribal nation—are regarded as relatives, and marriage within the same clan is forbidden.

The marriage of William and Elizabeth Parker was a long and successful one. Several of their seven children, six boys and one girl, proved to live up to the promise of their "noble birth," achieving notable success in both their own community and the new world of the European Americans. None of them, though, would achieve more fame or live a more colorful—and sometimes challenging life—than Elizabeth and William's middle child named Ha-sa-no-an-da, or Leading Name. All seven of the children were sent to the mission school to become educated in the European style. The Parkers, like Elizabeth's famous great-uncle, were well aware of the importance of gaining that type of education. It was not just for personal advancement but for the survival of their people.

Red Jacket put it plainly in one of his eloquent orations:

Unite, my brethren! Only by holding together in one great purpose, that of holding your lands, can we defeat the desire of land-grabbers to take all we have. Never mind the differences in religious belief. We are free to believe what we wish, and let the Great Spirit decide in his time what is right. Let us have schools as planned and

let our parents decide whether their children shall attend here or at Tuneassa where the good Quakers teach.

Red Jacket's most prized possession was a huge silver peace medal, presented to him by President George Washington in 1792. Of all the United States presidents, George Washington was held in the highest esteem because it was felt that he dealt honestly with the Indians. Thus, that medal had special meaning. In the 1825 painting *Red Jacket, Seneca Chief* by Charles Bird King, the old man is wearing the Washington medal. And it can be seen in other portraits of the great Native orator.

THE PEACE MEDAL, A LARGE OVAL OF SILVERPLATE ENGRAVED WITH AN IMAGE OF PRESIDENT GEORGE WASHINGTON SHAKING RED JACKET'S HAND. ON THE BACK OF THE MEDAL IS A STYLIZED SEAL OF THE UNITED STATES. 1792.

The medal, which shows a white man and an Indian sharing a pipe on one side and an American eagle on the other, became a symbol of more than just friendship between white and Indian. It became a symbol of the power of its holder to speak for the Seneca. On his death, the Red Jacket medal, as it came to be known, was passed down to Chief Jemmy Johnson.

Although Ha-sa-no-an-da was only two years old when his great-great-uncle died in 1830, the shadow cast by the great orator's life and words fell upon him. Red Jacket and his medal would always occupy an honored and special place in the heart of that young man, who would become the best known of the runners for his people.

But it was not as Ha-sa-no-an-da that the middle child of the Parker family became best known. By the early nineteenth century, many Senecas had adopted European names. Ha-sa-no-an-da's last name was Parker, the same as his parents. His first name, though, came from another source. It was Ely—pronounced, he always said, to rhyme with freely. It came from Baptist minister Elder Ely Stone, who was teaching at the mission school at Tonawanda.

And by that name of Ely Parker, the boy with the Seneca name of Ha-sa-no-an-da would come to occupy a unique and special place in American history.

THE RAINBOW DREAM

That the mysterious hieroglyphics on the beautiful face of the bow of the covenant was an assurance to her that the son to be born of her would "be learned and good" is beyond my ken. The vision was beautiful and heavenly divine . . .

—ELY S. PARKER, FROM A LETTER
DATED JANUARY 11, 1887

Dreams occupy an important place in all Native American cultures. Among the Iroquois and such nearby nations as the Wendats, or Hurons, the significance of dreams as prophecy and for spiritual guidance was enormous. This remained so after most Iroquois families had become practicing Christians—some as early as the seventeenth century. Missionaries of the various (and often competing) Christian sects could be found on every reservation.

Dream sharing, in which a dreamer would relate what she or he dreamed, was common, often followed by some action on the part of the dreamer—such as offering a feast to the community—to fulfill what the dream prophesied.

Such a prophetic dream would be forever linked to Ely Parker's life. It came to his mother about four months before he was born and so impressed her that she made a special visit to the Council House to relate it to a Djis-ga-da-ta-ha, a Dream Interpreter. She had dreamt that she was on the Buffalo Creek Reservation near a farm owned by a family named Granger. Heavy snow was falling, but suddenly the sky opened and even though it was winter, a rainbow appeared. Stretching from the reservation to the Granger farm, it was broken at its highest point in the sky. On the lower side of that rainbow were suspended signs like those over the stores of white men, with markings on those signs that she recognized—even though she could not read—as letters in the English alphabet.

What the dream interpreter then said to Elizabeth Parker was told to the writer Harriet Maxwell Converse by several Tonawanda elders. Converse, a close friend of Ely Parker in his later years, was regarded by the Senecas as a trustworthy defender of their interests.

"A son will be born to you," the Djis-ga-da-ta-ha said, "who will be distinguished among his nation as a peace-maker; he will become a white man as well as an Indian, with great learning; he will be a warrior for the pale-faces; he will be a wise white man but will never desert his Indian people nor lay down his horns as a great Iroquois chief; his name will reach from the east to the west, the north to the south, as great among his Indian family and the pale-faces. His sun will rise on Indian land and set on the white men's land. Yet the ancient land of his ancestors will fold him in death."

If that was, indeed, the dream that Ely's mother had, it certainly held elements of prophecy. One further part of that dream—that the rainbow was broken at its highest point—would prove to be eerily accurate.

Ely Parker himself, though, had little patience with prophecy or predestination playing any part in his life. In a skeptical letter dated January 11, 1887, when he was fifty-nine, he responded to Converse's reporting of that dream vision with the following:

I must . . . right here, disclaim any knowledge of my dear mother's dream, or vision, at a certain period of my pre-existence, or advent, into this world of troubles. The

"rainbow" business was rather an indiscreet interjection at so early a period of my affairs, and its influence and effects cannot with any degree of positiveness be explained or interpreted at this distance of time. It is possible that I may then have been impressed with that variegated and kaleidoscopic character of mind and fortune which thus far in my life has been my lot.

The exact day Ely was born, as was the case with most Seneca births at the time, was not recorded. His birth almost took place on the Buffalo Creek Reservation, the place the Senecas called Do-sho-wey (Place of the Basswoods). Elizabeth and William had taken a wagonload of lumber to sell there. Rather than spending the night, Elizabeth had insisted they return to their home, some ten miles away, on the Tonawanda Reservation near Indian Falls in the town of Pembroke, Genesee County. There, the young couple's three previous sons welcomed a new baby brother.

Not knowing the exact day of his birth would lead Parker to compare himself to the little girl in the famous antislavery novel *Uncle Tom's Cabin* by Harriet Beecher Stowe. As he wrote in a letter from January 7, 1887:

I sometimes envy people with birthdays and who can proudly point to some day of the year that passes over them as the day of all days most consequential to them. For remember, I am akin to Topsy who never had a birthday, never was born, and only growed up [sic]; my birthday which occurred sometime "in the course of human events" was never recorded in any book of man, hence I take the liberty of being neither elated nor depressed on any special day of the year and I know not whether I am old or young. I love all the days of the year alike, and can claim any one or all of them as my birthdays. Can any one be more blessed, and also more unfortunate?

The quote typifies Ely Parker's complex intelligence and sense of humor. Not only does he refer to the book that some say was a catalyst for the American Civil War, in which he played a very visible part, he also quotes—playfully—from the Declaration of Independence, as he declares his own independence from a birth date. The brilliance he showed in his later school years as a debater and orator with full mastery of the English language is very much in evidence.

Although we know he was first named Ha-sa-no-an-da, there has been some disagreement about its meaning. Usually translated as "Leading Name," its literal meaning is "Coming to the Front." In another quite different explanation of that Seneca name of Ely's, his grand-nephew Arthur C. Parker would claim it meant "The Reader" and was given to Ely by a teacher after he had displayed unusual scholarship.

Whether the Reader, Leading Name, or Coming to the Front, the name of Ha-sa-no-an-da would, like his mother's dream, reflect the life to be led by Ely Samuel Parker.

HA-SA-NO-AN-DA.
A YOUNG ELY S.
PARKER. DATE
UNKNOWN.

THE WHITE MAN'S SCHOOLS

Beginning at a very early date after the whites had commenced the settlement of this country, persons who were styled missionaries were sent out among all the Indian tribes that could be reached to Christianize them and teach them in book learning . . .

—FROM GENERAL ELY S. PARKER'S AUTOBIOGRAPHY

Ha-sa-no-an-da's early education was at home and in the surrounding woods, where he and his brothers and sister helped his mother in various activities, including making syrup in the early spring from the maple trees. In the tradition followed by most Native American families, he was encouraged to listen—especially to lesson stories—to observe, and, in a hands-on fashion, to learn by doing.

Further, whatever discipline he experienced was, by western standards, highly permissive. Physical punishment—or even speaking harsh words to your children—was regarded as deviant behavior. Handsome Lake was merely repeating the practices of countless Seneca generations when he said in the Good Message:

Now this is the way obtained by the Creator: Talk slowly and kindly to children and never punish them unjustly.

However, scaring children for their own good was and remains an essential part of indigenous child-rearing traditions throughout the continent. The traditional stories that the young Ely heard included tales of such monsters as giants made of stone, greedy flying heads hungry to devour anyone unlucky enough to be seen by them, and cannibal skeletons. Yet, in every case, if someone was calm enough and resourceful enough, even a small child might escape or even defeat such terrible beings. A quick-thinking boy named Skunny Wundy managed to overcome one stone giant after another. A quick-thinking woman turned the flying head's greed against itself. And a woman defending her baby escaped the clutches of the cannibal skeleton that had devoured her lazy husband, who ignored her advice. Such tales taught Seneca children not only that the world was full of danger, but also that those who'd listened well to the wisdom of their elders might navigate their way through its perils safely. Or perish if they were foolish.

Elizabeth Parker was, by all accounts, not only a beautiful woman but a strong and independent one. Throughout most of the year, the Parker family lived in frame houses like those of their white neighbors. But in the late winter, at the time of maple-sugaring, she and her children lived in the forest in the bark-shingled cabins built by her husband, William, in each of her several stands of sugar maple trees. Her children were never afraid while with her in the forest because "she had an ax and was a very good shot with either a gun or a bow. She always had both with her, and would shoot rabbits, coons, big birds and other game as well as any man."

If Ely had remained with his family, his life—and that of the Tonawanda Senecas—would have been a very different one. Neither of his parents could speak English fluently and although he might have become as fine an orator in Seneca as his great-great-uncle Red Jacket, his words would likely have had little effect outside the Native community. However, a traditional life—even one lived within the new confines of being a minority in their own homeland—was not to be the lot of Ha-sa-no-an-da.

By the time of Ely's childhood, the Iroquois nations had been dealing with Europeans for two centuries. They had traded, fought, and engaged in diplomacy with the Dutch, the French, and the English. Now they found themselves surrounded by the new, powerful American nation. Skilled diplomats, they understood that they could no longer rely on military force to protect themselves and their remaining lands. But, if they had trusted representatives who could speak for them—in the Americans' own language—they would be better served. Many of the most respected and influential leaders of the Senecas, not only Red Jacket but also his archrival Handsome Lake, believed this. None said it more directly than did Handsome Lake in the Good Message:

> Now another message to tell your relatives.
>
> This concerns education. It is concerning studying in English schools.
>
> Now let the Council appoint twelve people to study, two from each nation of the six. So many white people are about you that you must study to know their ways.

Although not a western-educated man himself, Ely's father had enough experience with the white man's world to understand the wisdom of Handsome Lake's words. So it was that Ely Parker found himself sent to the nearby Baptist Missions' boarding school, on the Buffalo Creek Reservation in New York, where he was one of the forty Seneca students enrolled there. As he described it, it was

> . . . one of these mission stations [that] existed near the Indian settlement where my parents lived. This station was conducted on the manual labor system, where the boys were taught the rudiments of agriculture and the girls the elementary principles of housewifery. I was sent at a very early age to this mission. We received board and clothing free and also whatever merits and demerits the institution possessed. I acquired there all the rudiments of reading, geography, and arithmetic . . .

SENECA SCHOOL HOUSE [BUFFALO CREEK, NEW YORK], 1821, BY DENNIS CUSICK, SON OF CHIEF NICHOLAS CUSICK OF THE TUSCARORA IROQUOIS

KEEPING THE SABBATH: SENECA SCHOOL HOUSE, 1821, BY DENNIS CUSICK

The education he gained in those first years was minimal. English was the required language. However, since the students were all Senecas, virtually no English was spoken except during lessons. All their interactions outside the classrooms were in their native tongue. None of them gained real fluency in that foreign, second language. As Ely himself explained:

> I understood very little of the English language; as the school was composed entirely of purely Indian pupils, they all would persist in speaking their native language when among themselves and the little English they required was not of an adhesive character. It did not, therefore, take long for me to disgorge all the learning with which I had been crammed.

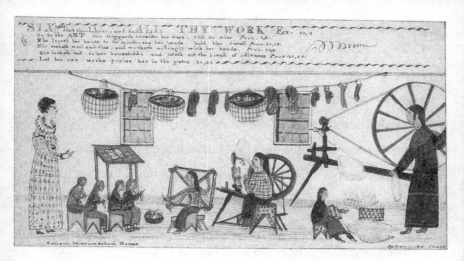

MRS. JAMES YOUNG, A MISSIONARY, TEACHING IROQUOIS GIRLS IN
THE SENECA SCHOOL, 1821, BY DENNIS CUSICK

Many years later, his niece, Laura Parker Doctor, the daughter of his brother Levi, would relate a telling family story about her uncle.

> One Sunday, the missionary found there was no
> interpreter. He looked everywhere to find one and after
> awhile he asked Grandfather if his boy could talk English
> and Grandfather said "Yes, a little." So Ely was called. . . .
> He was put on the pulpit stand and interpreted the
> sermon. Soon it was seen that he was speaking slower and
> still more slowly. Bye and bye [sic] he shut his eyes and
> then fell into a faint. The effort was too much, and it was
> his first attempt to speak in public . . .

At some point after that embarrassing incident, when he was around the age of ten, Ely decided he should go to the Six Nations Reserve to learn the ways of the forest that had always been a part of every Seneca boy's education. At Tonawanda they were hemmed in by white people who claimed ownership of the lands that had belonged to his people only a generation ago. The forests were devoid of game animals. The streams had been dammed and held few fish.

There was no way he could learn the old skills of hunting, fishing, and woodland survival close to home. However, at Grand River, around the town named for Joseph Brant, the woods had deer, the rivers trout, and the nearby lakes held salmon, sturgeon, and waterfowl. His parents agreed, and Ely set out for the lands of the Six Nations, traveling in the company of an older relative. In Brantford, Ely dove eagerly into his new life, perfecting himself in woodcraft in "the northern wilds of Canada."

Here I made good and rapid progress in archery, in the use of the fishing spear, the science of decoying the unsuspecting fish by means of the torchlight and the handling of the light birchbark canoe.

The two years he spent there must have been relatively carefree ones, away from the small reservation surrounded by white men eager to take their last few acres of land, no longer spending long hours inside a dreary classroom where he was forced to speak in a language that tangled his tongue. Family, though, has always been deeply important to Native people and it seems that William and Elizabeth Parker were especially loving and supportive of Ely and his siblings. Finally:

> **After one or two years, becoming surfeited with those heavy pursuits and being still very young, I began to yearn for my New York home and the companionship of my own beloved parents . . .**

So it was, that at the age of twelve or thirteen, he set out on his own to return "from the Canadian wilds to my New York home." The less than one-hundred-mile distance from Brantford to Tonawanda may not seem far to a modern traveler, who can make it in less than two hours by car. But back then, it was a walk of at least two or three days. It was during that long trek that an event occurred that seems to have been a turning point in young Ely's life—an unpleasant experience that led to an important realization.

Partway through his journey, in London, Ontario, he met two or three English officers who were traveling as he was toward "the city of Hamilton at the head of Lake Ontario." Ely's account of what transpired as they traveled together is too kind.

> It was natural that these officers should amuse themselves in some way to pass the time and tedium of travel. This they did at my expense, they all the time being under the impression that I did not understand or know the point of their jokes. The fact was that I did know just enough English to understand but I could not speak it well enough to enjoy their jokes. It was perhaps just as well that I could not. I was not injured and they had their fun . . .

It is all too easy to imagine the sort of "joking" that the young, sensitive Seneca boy endured as they walked together—being made fun of by men who assumed they were superior to a savage and never dreamed that his name would go down in history, while theirs would be forgotten. Or that their mocking his ignorance would actually inspire the taciturn young Tonawanda.

In perfect, almost Shakespearean prose, Parker explained decades later that:

> I bethought myself that perhaps it might be good for me did I thoroughly understand and speak the English language as well as to be able to read English books. I came to the determination that I would at least try the experiment.

And try it he did. Apparently, informing his parents that he wished to return to the Baptist Mission school was one of the first things he did after arriving home. There's little doubt that this pleased his father. William Parker was a stanch Baptist, by now a deacon and the church's treasurer. This second time around, Ely applied himself so well to his studies that his fluency in English was sufficient for the teachers at the mission to recommend him for a scholarship from the United States government's Indian Civilization Fund.

As a result, in September 1842, at the age of fourteen, Ely found himself at Yates Academy, twenty miles north of Tonawanda, as a full-time, tuition-free student.

For its time, Yates was highly progressive. Founded only a year before Ely arrived, at a time when relatively few women went beyond the first few years of elementary school, its student body was almost equally divided between the sexes with 119 "gentlemen" and 113 "ladies." Ely Parker was the first and only person of color. However, he soon found himself not only accepted by other students, but even struck up friendships with male comrades Lewis Blair, Reuben Warren, and Henry M. Flagler, deep connections that would last throughout his life. By all accounts, the young women of the school all found this tall, well-spoken, "exotic" young man interesting.

The school's faculty of three was led by a graduate of Williams

College, Benjamin Wilcox. Ely quickly became one of his favorites and would later describe Wilcox as a "most able, competent and conscientious teacher." The Seneca boy who had been tongue-tied to the point of unconsciousness while trying to interpret a church sermon and silent in the face of ridicule on his journey home from Canada seems to have taken quickly and easily to his new life within the walls of Yates. In less than a year, on April 18, 1843, he would be so competent as a public speaker that he could joke—in well-constructed prose—about the difficulty of thinking in English being too much for him.

> I have been engaged in translating the crooked Indian language into the English and the English back to the same and now I should like to have the society release me for I feel myself crazy, in getting the two languages mixed in my head.

Of course, that request was both ironic and far from the truth. By then, Ely Parker was a prized member of the Euglossians, one of the school's two literary societies. His orations always drew large, appreciative audiences. Mrs. Louise Bacheldor, a fellow Yates student who graduated in 1845, would recall Ely's physical presence and oratorical power in a letter published in 1875 in the *Buffalo Express*:

His was a noble, commanding form, tall, erect, broad-shouldered, and his straight, coal-black hair, high cheekbones and copper-colored complexion plainly told his origin. His genial affability won the respect of both teachers and schoolmates. No young man in school could compete with him in oratory.

There was also, for a time, a white girlfriend in the young Seneca student's life. Everyone took note of the fact that he was escorting her to evening meetings and lectures. Mrs. Bacheldor's letter to the newspaper told what happened next. It also demonstrated—as Arthur C. Parker, Ely's grand-nephew expressed it—"the prejudice of the day against Indian blood."

Although Parker possessed many traits that were commendable, he showed lack of discretion by falling in love with one of his fairest schoolmates who, strange to say, seemed to reciprocate his feelings . . . In time it was rumored that Parker was to take the young lady in question for a drive on the Fourth of July. Some credited the story, while others thought she, belonging to one of the most aristocratic families, would not disgrace herself and friends by riding out with an Indian. The Fourth of July came, when many were on the alert to know if the rumor was really true.

> Verandas were filled with people and even the street
> corners, when in a measure their curiosity was rewarded,
> as Parker went by with a grand livery and a negro driver.
> It was not long ere the splendid rig came rolling by and,
> sure enough, Mary was sitting at the side of Parker . . .
> The young lady soon went abroad for a long vacation.

Despite that romantic setback, Ely would recall his three years at Yates as some of the happiest in his life. But his time there was not uninterrupted. The Tonawanda chiefs had taken note of the young Ha-sa-no-an-da's progress. Their reservation was under constant attack from the speculators of the Ogden Land Company, which had already managed through yet another treaty in 1842 to gain approval of the purchase of the Buffalo Creek and Tonawanda reservations. None of the Tonawanda chiefs had approved this or signed the treaty. It would also be discovered later that all of the supposed signatures from the Buffalo Creek chiefs were forged. However, the Ogden Company was already making plans to sell the Tonawanda lands and distributing maps of proposed building lots. Someone fluent in English, able to translate from Seneca into the difficult language of those who sought to evict the Natives from their own lands, was desperately needed if they were to resist. In the past, non-Native translators had often proven themselves not only unreliable but susceptible to bribes from the Ogden Land Company. This time, the translator had to be one of their own.

Translating things for his people was nothing new for Ely Parker. He had already been involved in communicating with the highest level of the American government. One of the first documents he had translated and signed—at the age of fourteen—was a message to the president of the United States, John Tyler. From then on, every document sent by the Senecas to the state capital of Albany, or to Washington, was written and signed by him.

But now, at the age of sixteen, while only partway through his course of study at Yates, Ely Parker was called upon to serve as an interpreter and a runner for his people. His responsibility was not only to write documents; he was to travel as an interpreter at the side of Tonawanda leaders John Blacksmith and John Bigfire.

Thus, in April 1844, Ely found himself in Albany accompanying the delegation of Seneca chiefs. Having a little free time, he decided to visit one of those places not to be found anywhere near his home—a bookstore. There, while browsing eagerly through more books than he had ever seen in one place, he met someone who would, in the most dramatic fashion, change his life.

6

A MEETING IN ALBANY

As a youth, my people voted me a genius and loudly
proclaimed that Hawanneyo had destined me to be
their saviour and they gave public thanksgiving for the
great blessing they believed had been given them, for
unfortunately just at this period they were engaged in an
almost endless and nearly hopeless litigated contest for
their New York homes and consequently for their very
existence.

—FROM AN UNDATED LETTER BY ELY PARKER

ewis Henry Morgan came to Albany in April 1844 looking for
Indians—although perhaps not living ones. Born in 1818, and
a partner with his Union College classmate George F. Danforth
in a notably unsuccessful law firm, Morgan, along with his family,
had an interesting connection with the Iroquois. His grandfather,
Thomas Morgan, had been a Continental soldier in the Revolution-
ary War. He was lured from his home in Connecticut to move west

to the Finger Lakes region in New York where the dispossession of the Cayuga people following the war had opened up five million acres for white settlers. Whether he purchased the land on which he settled from the Cayugas, or was one of the many Continental soldiers granted formerly Indian land, is not known. What is certain is that he, his wife, and their three sons ended up with a large farm near the town of Aurora on Cayuga Lake.

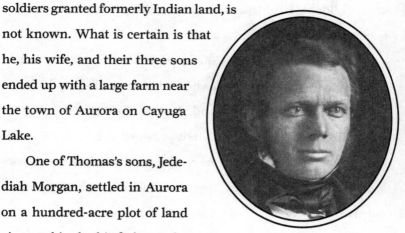

LEWIS HENRY MORGAN

One of Thomas's sons, Jedediah Morgan, settled in Aurora on a hundred-acre plot of land given to him by his father. Jedediah was a man of many accomplishments. He was not only a successful farmer, with large herds of cattle and sheep. He was also the inventor and manufacturer of a new plow, designed to dig long, deep, efficient furrows in the soil that had once been gently planted by Native farmers. Wealthy and respected, a member of the Masons, and the founder of the first Masonic Lodge in Aurora, he also was elected a New York State senator.

Lewis Henry Morgan was one of Jedediah's children. From his

earliest years he exhibited a passion for knowledge. He was more interested in delving into books than tilling the earth.

Apparently, Jedediah noticed and approved of his young son's bookishness. When Jedediah died in 1826, he left land to all his other children. His bequest to Lewis, however, was money to be used specifically for his education.

And use it Lewis Henry Morgan did. After elementary school he went to Cayuga Academy, where his course of study included Greek, Latin, mathematics, and rhetoric. In 1838, at the age of twenty, using those education funds provided by his late father, he entered Union College. There he continued his study of the classics at an accelerated rate, graduating with a baccalaureate degree after only two years.

In addition to gaining a higher education, Morgan came away from Union College with a new passion—one for secret societies. The Baptist president of Union, Eliphalet Nott, had forbidden such organizations and regarded the Bible as the first, last, and only guide for young men. But the students of Union paid no heed to that rule, founding numerous fraternities. It was one of those secret brotherhoods, the Kappa Alpha Society (which exists to this day, the oldest undergraduate fraternity in America), that Morgan joined in 1839.

That taste of fraternal life at Union College was not enough for Morgan. In 1841, a year after his graduation, he and some of his friends in Aurora founded their own secret brotherhood, naming it the Gordian Knot. The name came from the famous story about Alexander the Great. Upon reaching Phrygia with his army in the fourth century BC, he was shown a complicated tangle of seven knots and informed that whoever could solve it would be the ruler of Asia. Many had tried and, before the arrival of the young Macedonian, all had failed. According to the legend, Alexander simply sliced it in half with his sword.

Morgan's Gordian Knot, apparently begun as a sort of literary society, did not last that long. Within a year, Morgan and his friends had, as Morgan put it, cut the knot. Rather than ancient Greeks, they were now interested in Indians. Renamed and refocused, their fraternity was now the Grand Order of the Iroquois. They even managed to find a Seneca phrase that they adopted as the name of their lodge and used during their private rites: *We-yo-ha-yo-de-za-de Na Ho-de-no-sau-nee*: "They who live in the home of the dwellers of the Long House." Although none of those young white men seemed to have seen the irony of it, the focus of the Grand Order was on the history and culture of those departed nations upon whose stolen soil all of their white families had built their wealth.

The members of Morgan's society threw themselves into it with the zeal of present-day historical reenactors. They gave themselves Indian names, organized into tribes as Mohawks, Oneidas, Onondagas, Cayugas, and Senecas. They wore their own versions of Indian clothing at their yearly parades through Aurora and tried to learn the languages of the Five Nations. Having obtained permission to use the upper floor of the Masonic Temple in Aurora for their meetings, they created a secret rite called Inindianation to transform new members spiritually into Iroquois.

As silly as all this may sound (especially to a modern-day Native American), Morgan and his fellow lodge members were deeply devoted to finding out all they could about the former inhabitants of New York—the elusive "vanishing redmen," as romantic writers were describing Indians. Serious research into Iroquois history and culture, especially on the part of Lewis Henry Morgan, was important to them. Morgan made research trips to Albany, where detailed information on Indian treaties could be found in the state files. On one such trip, in April 1844, Morgan found himself in an Albany bookstore. As he wandered its aisles, looking for anything to do with Indians, he turned a corner and could not believe his eyes at what he saw.

There before him was a young man who—from his brown skin,

straight black hair, and facial features—had to be an Indian. Filled with excitement, Morgan barely managed to control himself. As he later wrote of the encounter: "To sound the war whoop and seize the youth might have been dangerous, but to let him pass without a parley would have been inexcusable."

Morgan struck up a conversation, halting at first until he realized the young man was fluent in English. It was, of course, Ely Parker. Morgan soon discovered, to his delight, that this well-spoken lad was one of the very people he'd been emulating and imitating. Not only that, Parker politely answered every question Morgan asked him. He was seventeen years old. His Seneca name was Ha-sa-no-an-da. He had become fluent while attending school at Yates Academy, where he was still a student. He had only taken a break from school at the request of his people, the Tonawanda Senecas, who needed a translator to accompany a delegation to meet with Governor William C. Bouck.

It is very likely that when Morgan described his Grand Order of the Iroquois, Ely realized this well-dressed young white man might be of use to him and the Tonawanda cause. The image of Native Americans being naive in their dealings with the European world is far from true. There is a long history of Native people flattering, "adopting," and bringing into their communities influential white people who were fascinated by Indians. While such relationships often developed into warm friendships, there was also a clear understanding on the part of Native Americans that these non-Natives could be valuable allies.

So, Ely suggested that the Indian hobbyist might want to meet his "grandfather," Sose-ha-wa, who was the leader of that Seneca delegation. Truly one of the most important Tonawanda leaders of that time, he was, as Ely described him in English, "the great high priest of the entire Six Nations." His grandfather was now resting, Ely explained, but perhaps Mr. Morgan would like to visit them that evening?

Needless to say, Morgan leaped at the opportunity and showed up promptly at the appointed time. His head must have been spinning as he was warmly welcomed by the delegation, who all seemed pleased to meet someone so deeply interested in them. Sose-ha-wa, "a fine-looking old man in his 67th year," was traditionally dressed and wearing a large silver medal. Morgan immediately recognized it from portraits as the famous medal given to Red Jacket by George Washington.

Each day from then on, while the delegation was in Ska-nen-ta-teh—the "Beyond the Pines," as the Iroquois have always called Albany—Morgan visited them. He took detailed notes as they answered question after question, sometimes correcting his mis-conceptions. To his credit, Morgan accepted their gentle criticism. By their last day together, the twenty-six-year-old Morgan had decided three things that would change both his life and the life of the young man he had just met.

First of all, he would continue to work with these amazing people, especially Ely, to learn all he could, visiting them in their homes on the reservation. He would (and did) keep up a detailed correspondence with Ely. Second, Ha-sa-no-an-da must become a member of the Grand Order of the Iroquois. And third, Morgan and the other members of the Grand Order should sponsor Ely's further education at the same Cayuga Academy in Aurora that they had attended. That last objective would serve a double purpose. Not only would it better the fine young Indian Morgan had grown to like immensely during their few days together; it would make Ely readily accessible to Morgan and the other members of their imita-tion Indian league.

A HIGHER
EDUCATION

After remaining nearly two years at this institution, I changed
my camping ground to Central New York, entering another
academy then venerable in years . . . Cayuga Academy at
Aurora, near Auburn, New York. About this time my people
were becoming deeply involved in trouble with their white
neighbors. As had already been the case, the Indians were in
the way of the march of civilization. The land they occupied
was rich and the white man needed it for his own use.

—FROM GENERAL ELY S. PARKER'S AUTOBIOGRAPHY

By the fifth decade of the nineteenth century, the Tonawanda
Senecas, though far from being assimilated, had adopted
many aspects of European American culture. They no longer
lived in large elm bark–covered longhouses with other members
of their clans. They resided in individual log cabins and frame
dwellings. The men were farmers, and many, with their families,
attended the Baptist church that also operated a small school on

the reservation. Their everyday dress was like that of their white neighbors—though they would adopt more colorful and traditional garb on special occasions.

They were, however, vastly outnumbered by the whites who sought to take their remaining land. A census conducted in 1845 by Henry Rowe Schoolcraft counted 505 Native people on the twenty-square-mile reservation. Schoolcraft was widely regarded at the time as the expert on Indians. The author of numerous books and papers on "the Indian," his wife, Jane Johnston, was mixed-race Ojibwe and taught her husband the Ojibwe language and many of the Native legends he later published. If Schoolcraft said something about the Tonawandas, the scholars of the day agreed, then it must be so.

In October 1845, when Morgan (and others of his faux Indians) visited Tonawanda for the first time, he managed to look beyond the seemingly European surface. He sympathized and decided to side with their struggle to retain their land. As Ely translated, Morgan listened eagerly to their answers to his questions about clans, customs, and the organization of the Great League, constantly taking notes. It was the beginning of Morgan's lifelong commitment to Native American culture. It was also the seed of a seminal volume in American ethnology—a book, thanks to Ely Parker and his family, that presented something much closer to a Native point of view than anything published before it. In point of fact, the young Seneca was more coauthor than informant. Although other members of Morgan's Indian club, which had readily accepted Ha-sa-no-an-da as an honorary member, fell away, Morgan visited Tonawanda again and again.

Meanwhile, having completed his studies at Yates, Ely Parker entered Cayuga Academy in Aurora, New York, that same October of 1845. His time at Yates seems to have prepared him well because he had no trouble in any of his subjects, including Greek and Latin. Being an Indian did make things challenging for him socially. Cayuga Academy was a much less accepting place for an Indian than Yates had been. But even there he managed to overcome—one way or another.

As he explained in a letter to his Yates friend Rueben Warren, "I have generally been used well. Much better than I expected, coming here an entire stranger. Once or twice I have been severely abused. But I returned blow for blow with savage ferocity."

On the debating stage, he proved more than equal to the challenge, including when one of his opponents tried to characterize Indians as godless savages.

"The Indian," Ely countered with typically poetic rhetoric,

"sees the great Spirit in the strong hurricane—he hears his whispers in the gentle zephyrs of evening—he studies Him in the thunder cloud, and views Him as he darts through the heavens in his electrical cars and humbly bows with reverence to his loud callings from the skies."

Soon, Ely was enjoying his new surroundings. His room overlooked Cayuga Lake, a place well known to his ancestors, as the numerous relics he found as he explored the hills around the campus attested. He was respected and praised by his teachers. The principal of Cayuga Academy described him as "a close student and an apt scholar."

Plans were also underway, with the aid of their friend Lewis Henry Morgan, for other members of the Parker family to come to Cayuga. Money had been raised from members of Morgan's Iroquois Order to support Ely's younger sister, Ga-hah-no, whose English name was Carolyn (Carrie), and another Seneca girl from Tonawanda. They would arrive in January, making Ely no longer the only Indian in the school, where he was now enjoying such success that it seemed his next logical step would be a place in one of the prestigious eastern institutions of higher learning—perhaps his friend Morgan's alma mater, Union College, or even Harvard.

8

AN INDIAN IN WASHINGTON

For many years I was a constant visitor at the State and Federal capitals either seeking legislative relief or in attendance at State and Federal courts. Being only a mere lad, the pale-faced officials with whom I came in contact, flattered me and declared that one so young must be extraordinarily endowed to be charged with the conduct of such weighty affairs.

—ELY PARKER, FROM AN UNDATED LETTER TO HARRIET CONVERSE

By that January of 1846 Ely had adapted well to life at Cayuga Academy. He was eighteen years old. But settled as his life was there, it was the opposite for his people at home in Tonawanda. The struggle of the Senecas to avoid eviction had been heating up. Morgan and his Grand Order of the Iroquois circulated petitions asking the government to set aside the treaties of 1838 and 1842 that "sold" Tonawanda. Those petitions were signed by thousands of New Yorkers as well as three United States senators. Ely, himself, spent a great deal of time gathering signatures, traveling from Tonawanda to Ithaca, Syracuse, and other parts of the state.

The next step (one he did not look forward to because it would interrupt his education) was to once again accompany a delegation of Tonawanda chiefs as their translator. Chiefs John Blacksmith and Isaac Shanks were chosen. Chief John Blacksmith was the leading "sachem" (an Algonquin term for a chief that was widely used in English to refer to those men the Iroquois called royaners) of the Seneca nation and bore one of the fifty names passed down from the founding of the Great League. He was Do-ne-ho-ga-wa, or Open Door, the symbolic keeper of the western door.

Chief Isaac Shanks, an equally experienced leader, was the second delegate. Although both Seneca elders were deeply respected among their own people, neither could speak English. Further, this time instead of merely going to Albany, their destination would be the far-off nation's capital—Washington, D.C.

So, in February 1846, Ely Parker made his first, brief trip to Washington. He'd already spent most of the month of January away from school on a mission to Albany. However, because his services were needed, he grudgingly accepted the responsibility yet again.

It was not a pleasant experience for him. "Oh, how I do long for my native woods," he wrote in his diary soon after arriving in Washington. "This place has no charms for me; the choicest wisdom of this great American republic gather here, but what care I for that. It is from this place the decrees have emanated, dooming my kin to the grave."

The only good thing about that trip for Ely, it appears, was how brief it was. The delegation met no success at all and soon returned to Tonawanda.

Despite that romantic assertion about longing for his "native woods" (which were then being cut down by white timber pirates), what Ely seems most to have longed for was a chance to continue his education. Upon returning home he'd found a letter waiting for him. Plans were being made for him to attend Wilson Collegiate Institute—to prepare him to enter Williams College. But that was not to be. Less than two weeks after returning home, the chiefs called on his services again.

Another delegation was being sent to Washington. This time they were guaranteed a meeting with President James Polk and William Marcy, the secretary of war, who was the person in the government in charge of Indian Affairs. Once again, Chiefs Blacksmith and Shanks would lead the delegation. And, just as before,

UNITED STATES CAPITOL, WASHINGTON, D.C., EAST FRONT ELEVATION, CIRCA 1846. PHOTOGRAPH BY JOHN PLUMBE.

the entire responsibility for communicating with the highest-ranking leaders of the United States would rest on the eighteen-year-old shoulders of Ely Parker.

This trip turned out to be far different for him. On March 19, when the delegation met the president, Polk greeted him warmly. "Hurra for Polk! He is a fine and pleasant gentleman," Ely would write to a friend. "He is very talkative and inclined to be merry. That's the man for me."

Things were not as pleasant for the two chiefs. The president refused to discuss their case without the secretary of war being present and Marcy was a hard man to pin down. Days passed, during which Ely toured Washington on his own, familiarizing himself with the city that—though he did not know it at the time—would be a central part of his future. It took until March 25 for them to get a meeting with the secretary of war. They presented their petitions and their case. They opposed the treaties. If their land was sold they would, as in Red Jacket's story of the man on the end of the log, have no place to go. They did not want to move west. They wanted a new treaty that would allow them to remain on their land. Though, like the president, the secretary of war was sympathetic; he said that the matter could only be resolved in the Senate.

Their petition was finally presented to the Senate on April 1. The Seneca delegation—through Ely—made their case. But Joseph Fellows, the representative of the Ogden Land Company, was there as well. The treaties had been ratified and were now the law of the land. The appraisers had valued the worth of the Tonawanda Reservation at $15,018.36. Fellows deposited that amount with the government, though the Senecas objected. Now, Fellows said, all that remained was to remove the Indians. To some, it seemed to be over, but not to the Tonawandas, who continued to refuse the settlement.

At this point the Tonawanda Senecas hired an influential and highly respected lawyer, William Linn Brown of Philadelphia. Meanwhile, more and more petitions supporting the Indians were sent to Washington, including a "memorial" delivered to the nation's capital in person by Lewis Henry Morgan. Ely himself embarked on a series of trips. To Albany to ask the governor to protect his people. To New York City to solicit expert testimony from Henry Schoolcraft. Back to Albany and then to New York City again, where he tried to meet with their new lawyer, William Linn Brown, who was becoming hard to find.

The elusive lawyer had made a secret trip to Cuba, supposedly for the State Department, to meet with Antonio López de Santa Anna, the president of Mexico—which would soon be at war with the United States. Though Brown had gladly accepted the Senecas' retainer, they were low on his list of priorities.

Once again, Ely returned to Washington—where the Seneca delegation was without their absent lawyer. When the two chiefs decided to return to Tonawanda—where Indians were now being arrested for trespassing on their own land—Ely remained in the capital. On May 18, 1846, he presented a letter from the Tonawandas to Polk, asking the government to protect the Indians, who were now being threatened by armed men hired by the Ogden Land Company, some carrying "as many as four pistols each."

In his meeting with the president, Ely brought to bear all the rhetorical skills he had honed at Yates and Cayuga when people

71

packed the halls to hear him speak. He pointed out that his people were not seeking revenge against those taking their land but asking for the treatment promised them in the Treaty of Peace and Friendship the United States signed with the Six Nations in 1796.

We have ever felt a strong friendship for the people of the United States. We love its republican institutions. We have shed our blood in common with the good citizens of the United States, in the defense of her rights, and all we desire and ask now, is that our love of peace and the great friendship we have for the United States may not suffer by the conduct of individuals—unprincipled white men; but in the spirit of that Treaty which we hold as almost sacred we desire to establish a firmer friendship which shall ever remain unbroken, by amicably adjusting our present difficulties.

Perhaps his words had some effect, for Polk referred the matter to William Medill, his commissioner of Indian Affairs. Medill had a poor opinion of Indians as a whole, considering them to be ignorant, degraded, lazy, and in need of being civilized. However, he, too, may have been impressed by the words of this eloquent young Seneca. The executive branch, Medill said, would take no action against the Indians while the case was still undecided in the Senate.

As weeks and then months went by, Ely remained in Washington, staying in a pleasant rooming house on funds provided by the Tonawandas. Although frustrated about the lack of progress in the case for his people, he was now finding the nation's capital enjoyable. His initial impression of it having no charms for him was changed. "There is no one, I believe," he wrote of his time in Washington, "who enjoys himself half so well."

In that time when the nation's borders were constantly being pushed west, delegations of other Indians were a common sight. He met John Ross, the principal chief of the Cherokee Nation that had been removed to Indian Territory. And his response on seeing a group of Indians from the Texas border reflects both his sense of humor and how far his own Seneca people were now removed from the ways of those "wild" Indians.

They look wild enough to throw anyone of a delicate constitution into the fits. If I had such Indians at the north, I could whip the Ogden Company & all their accomplices in less time than you could say "Jack Roberson." They have as you may suppose very little clothing to cover their bodies, which of course would make the virtuous portion of the fairer sex blush . . .

73

Ely also busied himself with sightseeing, visiting the national fair and Mount Vernon, listening to debates about the war with Mexico, attending Odd Fellows meetings, while waiting for their missing lawyer to reappear.

At one point, while walking along a street in Washington, a carriage pulled up beside him.

"Would you like a ride, Mr. Parker?" the well-dressed woman in the carriage asked him.

"Yes, Mrs. Polk, thank you kindly," Ely replied, and soon found himself riding about the city in the company of the first lady of the land.

Meanwhile, in more ways than one, the Tonawanda Reservation was in turmoil. Some Senecas were seriously considering taking the Ogden offer. Others were now criticizing Ely, even accusing him (falsely) of accepting bribes to work against their interests.

His brother Da-ah-de-a, whose English name was Nicholas (Nic), was now a student himself at Cayuga. He wrote Ely about the mood at Tonawanda. "Some of our people here," he told Ely in a letter dated June 14, 1846, complain that you are "nothing but a little boy, not old enough yet to attend to such a great business."

74

There is an old saying among the Six Nations that was as true then as it is in the present day. Anyone who stands up to be a leader must have a skin seven thumbs thick to withstand the criticism that will inevitably come their way. Perhaps Ely had that in mind, for he did not give up, even though his expense money was now running low.

Finally, on July 14, Brown returned from his mission to Cuba. However, the Senate committee was occupied with other matters. On August 6, without considering the Tonawanda case, the Senate adjourned till their next session and Ely headed back home to the reservation. His aim, though, was not to stay there. His time away had made the life there seem restricted and unrewarding. Either going to college—if he could find a way to fund it—or seeking his fortunes in the West were the options he was now considering.

But, once again, the Tonawanda chiefs had need of him. Earlier in that year of 1846, a group of approximately 150 Tonawandas had decided to do as the government asked and relocate, accepting western lands offered to them in the distant Kansas territories. Within four months, half of them had died from the unhealthy conditions there. Fearful that this might be their fate as well, the Tonawanda chiefs asked Ely to return again to Washington to plead their case.

IROQUOIS INDIANS IN KANSAS

He ended up doing it alone. Although Ely had become quite comfortable in white settings, Washington was not a place the elderly chiefs liked to go.

Ely arrived back in Washington on Friday, January 1, 1847. He was just in time for the annual New Year's reception at the White House. Modern ideas of security and protecting a president did not exist then. Wearing tribal garb, Ely made his way to the White House. At eleven in the morning, the building was crammed with visitors—so many that some were exiting by climbing out one of the ground-floor windows. No one tried to either stop or question the young man who was clearly an American Indian by his colorful attire.

The old saying that "clothes make the man," was one that Ely always lived by. One of his first purchases after reaching Cayuga Academy had been a fine frock coat. With only one notable exception, every photo of Ely Parker from his teenage years on shows him in either a military uniform or a suit. However, like all of the Indians who came on diplomatic business to the nation's capital, when meeting government representatives Ely dressed in a more traditional way, one that would make him stand out as a "real Indian"; the Red Jacket medal—loaned to him by his grandfather—hung proudly around his neck.

It had the desired effect. As Ely would ironically note, he was the object of a great deal of attention as everyone stared at him while he walked through the crowd. They might not have known exactly who he was, but "close inspection and my native costume soon assured them that it was a savage brave, who thus had the audacity to mingle with the nobility." Moreover, President Polk "instantly recognized me and very familiarly and courteously offered his hand."

In the weeks that followed, Ely visited senator after senator, pleading the Senecas' case. At first he did so alone. Then, when their lawyer, William Linn Brown, finally turned up, the two of them worked on their presentation to the committee. It seemed the tide was turning their way. But when the report was finally released on February 19, their hopes were swept out to sea. The committee agreed that the original treaty was fraudulent. However, annulling a treaty on any grounds would "tend to strongly unsettle the whole of our Indian policy."

Ely returned home with the disheartening news. The years of effort and the expenditure of thousands of dollars had failed to convince the United States Senate. However, rather than give up, the determined Tonawandas turned to the courts. They sued the Ogden Land Company over an incident in which Chief Blacksmith had been evicted from his own sawmill on the grounds that the company now owned the land.

Meanwhile, freed for now of his responsibilities as an envoy, Ely could finally turn again to plans for his own future.

9

A LAWYER, AN ENGINEER

They are represented as in a starving condition, and being about to land, an Indian has come forward offering them provisions of his bounty. Who now of the descendants of those illustrious pilgrims will give one morsel to the dying and starving Indian?

—ELY PARKER'S OBSERVATIONS IN 1848 ON A RELIEF IN SANDSTONE OF THE PILGRIMS IN THE U.S. CAPITOL'S ROTUNDA

What direction should he now go? He was nineteen years old, brilliant, more aware than most white youths his age of the possibilities that should be offered to such a well-spoken, energetic young man. But he was also still an Indian. He applied to Harvard, but even with a recommendation from his congressman, was not accepted. He sought employment as a clerk in the Indian office, asking Henry Schoolcraft to help him. Nothing came of that, either.

Then, it seemed, the perfect opportunity arose. William P. Angel, a young lawyer, had recently taken the position of federal Indian agent in Cattaraugus County in western New York. By then, Ely Parker's reputation was well known to anyone dealing with Indian affairs in the state. So it is not surprising that Angel asked Ely to assist him and his partner in their work with the Indians at their law office in Ellicottville, the county seat. In turn, Ely could study law with them. Ely leaped at the opportunity. He had already learned how important a knowledge of the law could be in his dealings with the state and federal governments. He'd seen the respect given to lawyers.

Although becoming a lawyer in the United States now entails years of education at the university level, in the nineteenth century, law was often learned "on the job." Abraham Lincoln, for example, was largely self-taught. With no more than twelve months of formal education, the future "Great Emancipator" Lincoln learned the law by working in an Illinois law office much like the one where Ely was now employed.

Ely turned out to be a gifted law student as he happily settled in to life in Ellicottville. Angel and his partner, Addison G. Rice, praised his work. The citizens of the town respected and liked him. He became a member of the Masons. Men's societies have always been an important part of Seneca life and the Masons were the most important such group in the white society of the time. Having already been a part of Morgan's lodge of white men playing Indians probably prepared him for this next step. Being a Mason meant being accepted into European America at a deeper level, providing significant political and social contacts. Ely's membership in this brotherhood would, in fact, be of crucial importance throughout the rest of his life. Moreover, he was not the first Iroquois to join ranks of the Blue Lodge, as Masonry was called, since Joseph Brant had risen high in their ranks a century before him.

It seemed as if his life was finally to be a settled one, away from the responsibilities to represent his people—and the harsh criticism he'd continued to receive from those Senecas who resented his position, abusing him "all but to death, charging me of intriguing with the Company."

What free time he had was taken up by other projects, for Ely continued to work with his friends and patrons Henry Schoolcraft and Lewis Henry Morgan. The two scholars were basing much of their ethnological research on the Senecas on information the young, deeply knowledgeable Indian was readily providing them. Like other writers who would follow them, they realized that no informant was more valuable than Ha-sa-no-an-da. Here was a man who not only had access to the traditions of his people, but was

LANDING OF THE PILGRIMS, 1620, RELIEF IN SANDSTONE BY ENRICO
CAUSICI, 1825, CAPITOL ROTUNDA, ABOVE EAST DOOR. THIS IS THE
RELIEF THAT ELY SAW WHILE REPRESENTING THE CHIEFS OF TONAWANDA
IN EARLY 1848.

more fluent in English than many for whom it was a first language.

There is little evidence that Ely had any time for romance during that period in Ellicottville. Aside from learning the rites of Masonry, he was devoting every waking minute to studying the law and acting as a primary ethnological source for his scholarly patrons. Yet it is possible that, as seemed to happen everywhere he went, the dashing young Indian was taken note of by the young ladies of the town. Perhaps, as at Yates, there might have been a woman in his life.

However, as had happened so often before, the chiefs at Tonawanda decided they needed Ely's help. And, as always, he could not refuse. So, early in 1848, he and Chief Isaac Shanks found themselves again in Washington. And, again as before, nothing came of their brief visit. The 29th Congress having expired the year before, their case would now be "new business" for the 30th Congress—later that year. "Go home," his friend Henry Schoolcraft advised, "and wait."

Ely's return to Tonawanda near the end of January did not have a happy beginning. On January 29, 1848, he was physically assaulted when he confronted a white man, Ichabod Walton. Walton and his crew were going on the reservation and stealing timber. Although Walton "did then and there beat strike wound and evil treat and other wrongs to the said Ely S. Parker," for once a white man did not go unpunished for ill-treating an Indian. Walton was charged by the district attorney, John Henry Martindale, and brought before a jury, where he was found guilty and fined. It must have seemed to Ely a welcome example of the power of the law he was now pursuing as a career, especially because a jury made up entirely of white men had

proven to him that "justice was blind" by finding in favor of an Indian.

It was also proof of how effective Martindale would be in working for the Tonawandas. From 1846 to 1861, he served as their lead attorney and he and Ely would work in an effective close partnership to prevent the dispossession of the Tonawanda Senecas. Born in Hudson Falls, New York, in 1815, he was a graduate of West Point and an engineer. Practicing law first in Batavia and then Rochester, he became known as one of the most capable and effective lawyers in New York State. A strongly built, erect man of medium height with black curly hair, described as "attractive and genial," Martindale was just the sort of lawyer Ely hoped to become.

JOHN HENRY MARTINDALE

For the first half of 1848, Ely buried himself in the study of the law. It seemed a foregone conclusion he would become a lawyer. His friends and family were already addressing him as "Ely Parker, Attorney and Counselor at Law," and he was, in the office of Angel and Rice, providing legal assistance to the Alleghany Senecas and Tuscaroras, as well as his own Tonawandas.

Although it has been stated in various places that Ely Parker studied law at Union College, that is almost certainly not true. Union has no record of his ever attending and his life was too busy for him to have been in residence there as a student. He was being taught all he needed to know about the legal profession by his work in the Ellicottville law firm. That work, however, came to an end when, in the summer of 1848, William Angel was discharged from his post as a subagent for the New York Indians and thus Ely's help was no longer needed. It was, apparently, a political decision. Petitions were circulated (with Ely's help) on Angel's behalf, but to no avail.

Though his work with Angel and Rice was done, Ely had been well enough prepared to take the bar exam and become a lawyer on his own. But it turned out there was a legal obstacle. Only a natural-born or a naturalized citizen of the United States could be admitted as an attorney. Even though no one was more "natural born" than a Native American, no Indian could be an American citizen. It was not until 1924 that an Act of Congress gave citizenship to American Indians.

Ely appealed to the courts to be allowed to take the bar exam and was turned down. His ambition to be a lawyer having ended, he considered seeking his fortune to the west in far-off Oregon. Once again, his friend Morgan stepped in. Rather than lose his youthful collaborator on the Iroquois project that had now turned into a substantial manuscript, he suggested Ely consider a career in engineering. Morgan could recommend him for a state job working on the new Genesee Valley Canal. He could start as an axman and learn the fundamentals of engineering on the job. There would be no legal barriers in his way and the state had a duty to employ educated Indians.

In early 1849, Ely began his new life in engineering, working on a four-man crew. At first his job only consisted of clearing lines of sight, but he worked hard and was, as always, a quick learner. The men he worked with were well educated and enjoyed teaching the quiet, likeable young Indian. They even took him to country dances with them, where one of their wives taught the bashful Ely, now twenty-one years old, how to dance. It was a pursuit he learned to love and he soon became the favored dance partner of a number of young ladies.

A story from the Ely S. Parker papers at the American Philosophical Society paints the picture of an increasingly sophisticated young man who had not forgotten the lessons of his youth. In a letter to one of his Yates friends, Ely recounted how he had been at a dance in the town of Ischua. When he awoke the next morning and looked out the window of the hotel where he'd spent the night, he saw deer tracks in the moist earth. Without any weapon, he followed those prints. There is an old, honored tradition among the Native people of the northeast of running down a deer, chasing it on foot until it tires and can go no farther, then—after thanking the deer for giving its life—killing it by covering its mouth and nose. That is what the young engineer-in-training did, bringing the deer back on his shoulders to share its meat with his fellow workers.

His first engineering job lasted ten months. During that time the Senecas' struggle to keep their land was continuing. Ely wrote letters on their behalf, but when a Seneca delegation attended the inauguration of the twelfth president, Zachary Taylor, in 1849, it was Ely's brother Nic who went to Washington as their interpreter.

Engineering—not unpaid diplomacy or the law—was now the chosen career path for Ely. In the spring of 1850, with the help yet again of Morgan (who was determined to keep his primary informant close), he accepted another engineering job in New York. His work would be in the office of the resident engineer for New York State Canals in Rochester, forty-five miles east of Tonawanda.

10

THE LEAGUE OF THE HO-DE-NO-SAU-NEE

At Red Jacket's death, in accordance with Indian custom, Red Jacket's medal was given by his relations, in the distribution of his personal effects, to one James Johnson, a favorite nephew of his, and at that time a young and promising chief.

—ELY PARKER, LETTER TO
GEO S. CONOVER, ESQ., MARCH 9, 1891

After his stays in Washington, adapting to life in a busy, growing city, such as Rochester, was not hard for Ely. Nor was his work in the canal office. The project he was working on was the enlarging of the Erie Canal. In those mid-nineteenth-century days before the modern networks of paved roads and the introduction of motorized vehicles, the Erie Canal and the other man-made waterways connected to it were vital to the success and expansion of eastern industries. Goods, livestock, and people could be transported swiftly and easily by barges and other boats. When construction on the long canal had begun in Rome, New York, on July 4, 1817, skeptics had called it "Clinton's Ditch" and "Clinton's Folly" after DeWitt Clinton, the then governor. But when it was completed in 1825, its success was immediate. It cut transportation costs by as much as 95 percent. The second longest canal in the world after the Grand Canal in China, its 363 miles carried commerce from the Hudson River near Albany to the Great Lakes near Buffalo.

ERIE CANAL BOAT, 1850

Ironically for Ely, that same canal had contributed to the population surge in the western part of New York that put such pressure on the Seneca reservations. By the time Ely began his canal work, the Buffalo Creek Reservation—which encompassed most of the land of present-day Buffalo—had been dissolved.

As always, Ely proved himself to be an incredibly quick learner. Soon he was no longer clearing brush, but holding the rod for the transitman, the surveyor whose job it was to record and make observations through a transit while laying out a project. Soon, Ely took on that more skilled position of surveyor as well. And, by the end of his first year, he had progressed from transitman to the lofty post of second engineer, one of those involved in planning and overseeing an entire project.

Two other pursuits also occupied Ely's time. The first was his work with Morgan. Not only was he helping him with the completion of his book, he and his ethnologist friend were gathering artifacts for the New York State Museum. Their travels took them from the Grand River reserve in Ontario to all the Iroquois communities in the state. Ely's grand-nephew Arthur C. Parker related a fascinating story about one of those relics in his biography of his famous great-uncle, *The Life of General Ely S. Parker*.

Among the rarer relics in the State collection is
Cornplanter's tomahawk. This beautiful relic of the days
now gone forever has an interesting history . . . It was sent to
a friend of [Cornplanter's] known as Canada. When Canada
died his widow preserved the heirloom which was widely
known and often looked at by the curious among the tribes.
When her cabin burned it was Ely Parker who rescued it
from the flames. To him it was part of family history, for
Cornplanter was the half brother of his great grandfather.

Once again, the tomahawk was threatened by fire.
When on March 29, 1911, the State Library and the
archaeological collections were destroyed by a disastrous
fire, the writer tore the tomahawk from the case where
it hung.

Perhaps the most interesting artifact that Ely Parker collected
during this period was one that he did not intend for any museum
collection. It was too deeply personal, for it linked him to his culture
and his role as a spokesman for his people in the deepest possible
way. It was the Red Jacket medal. Though Ely had been loaned it
on a regular basis for his many visits to the state and national capitals, it was regarded as the personal possession of his grandfather,
Jemmy Johnson. Johnson, as everyone knew, had inherited it as a
favorite nephew of his uncle Red Jacket. However, while Ely was

away from Tonawanda, at some point after 1849, his grandfather agreed to sell the medal to the New York State Museum. As soon as he heard of this, Ely sprang into action. He intercepted the medal and paid his grandfather the same amount he would have received from the museum.

The other thing occupying Ely's spare time was his continued advocacy for the Tonawandas, aided by his older brother Spencer, who had chosen to take the last name of Cone while at odds with his family as a young man, but had since reconciled with them. When Ely drafted a bill in March 1851, it was Spencer who delivered it to Albany as the official representative of his people.

Early 1851 saw a major milestone in Ely's life. Lewis Henry Morgan's book, *League of the Ho-de-no-sau-nee*, which owed most of its existence to Ely Parker and his family, was published. Just how deep that debt was could be seen in its opening pages. The frontispiece illustration is of two Senecas, meant to represent the people of the Six Nations. To the left is a fine-featured serious young woman. Her head tilted to the left, she is dressed in the embroidered cloth and leggings that had become formal wear for Iroquois women since the introduction of European fabrics. To the right is a well-muscled young man, also in traditional regalia. An embroidered sash around his neck and across his chest, a turban-like

GA-HAH-NO, CARRIE PARKER (LEFT), AND DA-AH-DE-A, NIC PARKER (RIGHT), WERE MODELS FOR THE FRONTISPIECE OF *LEAGUE OF THE HO-DE-NO-SAU-NEE*, 1851.

gustoweh on his head bears the single erect eagle feather that stands for the Seneca nation. In his hands is firmly held a decorated, quite formidable-looking war club. The look on his face, like that of the woman's, is that of a no-nonsense guardian. The two who modeled for that illustration—which captured their strength and personalities—were Ely's siblings Carrie and Nic.

If anyone doubted how much Morgan's book owed to his native collaborator, that doubt would have been dispelled by its dedication:

TO

H A S A NO NAN DA
(ELY S. PARKER)

A SENECA INDIAN

**THIS WORK
THE MATERIALS OF
WHICH ARE THE FRUIT OF
OUR JOINT RESEARCHES
IS INSCRIBED IN ACKNOWLEDGEMENT
OF THE OBLIGATION
AND IN TESTIMONY OF
THE FRIENDSHIP OF**

THE AUTHOR

There are many things about that unique book for which Morgan deserves credit. His gracious and grateful acknowledgment of the role played by his brilliant young Seneca friend is stated just as strongly in the book's brief preface where Morgan wrote:

It remains for the author to acknowledge his obligations to Ely S. Parker, Ha-sa-no-an-da, an educated Seneca Indian, to whom this volume is inscribed. He is indebted to him for invaluable assistance during the whole progress of the research, and for a share of the materials. His intelligence and accurate knowledge of the institutions of his forebears, have made his friendly service a peculiar privilege.

Another thing that made Morgan's book so groundbreaking— apart from his deep reliance on an actual living, cooperative, western-educated, and sophisticated informant—was its benevolent intention as stated in the preface's first sentence:

To encourage a kinder feeling towards the Indian, founded on a truer knowledge of his civil and domestic institutions, and of his capacities for future elevation, is the motive in which this book originated.

It's important to recognize the age in which this book was written. The United States was still deeply engaged in the seemingly endless wars against Native American nations that had begun in the seventeenth century. The destruction or dispossession of Indian nations in the service of the nation's "Manifest Destiny" to encompass the entire continent was a given. Indians were often seen as ignorant savages or even less than human. Morgan's book was a huge departure from that—even if he did see the Indian as being in need of "future elevation."

League of the Ho-de-no-sau-nee, which still remains in print, was truly a classic text. It attempted to look at a Native American culture on its own terms. Its uniqueness and strength are among the reasons why Morgan is often referred to as the father of American anthropology.

It is, of course, not perfect. Later writers have pointed out errors and omissions and criticized Morgan for the patronizing point of view that creeps in here and there. Despite his intelligence and his commitment to help Native Americans—a commitment that remained throughout his life—he was a white man of his time. He was also relying on a single individual, Ely Parker, and, to a lesser degree, Ely's family for nearly all his information. No single person, community, or even tribal nation could speak for the complex Six Nations, past or present. But what Morgan—and Ely—accomplished was truly amazing. It is a book that, even today, is a wonderfully detailed portrait of a unique confederacy of Native nations.

Late that spring of 1851, Chief John Blacksmith "walked on," a term still commonly used among Native people to refer to a person's passing from this life, taking the Sky Trail that leads to the place where the strawberries are always ripe. A new "grand sachem" had to be raised up to bear the name of Donehogawa. In a letter sent to Ely in July, Spencer expressed his confidence that Ely—now twenty-three years old—would be the one selected.

How could one so young be chosen for so lofty a position? It was not all that unusual then—nor is it now—for Iroquois men in their early twenties to be installed by the women of their clan as a representative to the Great League. These men were never chosen on the basis of a brief election campaign. Instead, an Iroquois leader was selected on the basis of how he'd shown himself to be. The women of his clan had observed Ely closely from the earliest years of childhood. They had recognized who among the young men had such qualities as generosity, patience, and careful decision making, qualities regarded as necessary to be a royaner—one of the fifty sachems, or chiefs. That choice was made not by secret ballot but by consensus. Although a council of chiefs would be held to formally announce who had been elected, the women of his clan would decide who would wear the deer horns that symbolized the office of a royaner.

However, the role of the women did not end when a royaner was chosen. The word *royaner* translates into English as "he makes a good path for the people to follow," and anyone holding that office was expected to live that way. Thus the clan mothers would continue to watch him, making sure he properly discharged his office. If he began to misbehave, they would warn him. If his bad behavior continued, they could remove him from his sachemship, take away his horns. Further, to be one of the fifty royaners, one had to be a man of peace. If he killed someone or simply went to war—which was the job of the war chiefs—he would forfeit his position.

Spencer's letter turned out to be accurate. On September 19, 1848, Ely Parker was called to attend a grand council meeting at Tonawanda. The gathering included the representatives of all Six Nations. Dressed in their formal regalia, the remaining forty-nine sachems were present from the Onondaga, Mohawk, Oneida, Cayuga, and Seneca nations. Although representatives of the Tuscaroras were present, because they had joined the Great League centuries after its original formation, they had no sachems. Instead they were "sheltered under the branches" of the Great League, which had given them sanctuary when they were driven by white men from their original homes in North Carolina.

After the fire that symbolized the heart of the Great League was kindled, the ancient Condolence Ceremony in honor of John Blacksmith, who had carried the title of Donehogawa, took place. The roll call of the original founders of the Confederacy was sung, not just as an expression of grief, but also as a way of lifting the grief from those who mourned Blacksmith's passing. A sachem's life might end, but his spirit lived on and his office would be taken up anew by the next chosen to represent his people.

At that council, a number of other men were raised up to lesser sachemships, becoming Pine Tree Chiefs (as Red Jacket had been); Faith Keepers, whose job it was to advise their sachem; or the war chiefs. One of those chosen as a war chief was Ely's brother Spencer.

Finally it was Ely's turn. He had, indeed, been chosen. He would no longer simply be Ha-sa-no-an-da. He would now be the new Donehogawa, the Open Door.

The flickering light of the council fire, the solemn, orderly procession of the chiefs dressed in ceremonial regalia, the singing of the roll call of the chiefs whose names had been chanted many hundreds of times before—all of this must have been tremendously moving to the young man whose life had been following such different roads. He must have felt himself connected to that long chain of Iroquois tradition, still unbroken despite all the odds against them. He heard spoken to him in his native tongue the same ancient words of advice he had translated into English for Morgan, words he would try to live by for the rest of his life:

ONE REAL AMERICAN

The thickness of your skin shall be seven spans—which
is to say that you shall be proof against anger, offensive
actions and criticism. Your heart shall be filled with
peace and good will and your mind filled with a yearning
for the welfare of the people of the Confederacy. With
endless patience you shall carry out your duty and your
firmness shall be tempered with tenderness for your
people. Neither anger nor fury shall find lodgement in
your mind and all your words and actions shall be marked
with calm deliberation.

There was, however, one part of that deeply ceremonial council
that was not traditional. It was also emblematic of the new world
that many of the Indian nations of the American continents had
now been attempting to navigate for three centuries or more. It was
the Red Jacket medal. Even though it was already in his possession,
having purchased it from his uncle, even though he had worn it on
countless occasions as a representative of his people, it was not until
this moment that Ely must have felt it was finally truly his.

As he expressed in a letter written forty years after the council:

At my installation as leading Sachem of the Iroquois
Confederacy in 1851, I was formally invested with it by
the master of ceremonies formally placing it about my

ELY CIRCA 1855,
WEARING THE RED
JACKET MEDAL

neck, the speaker remarking the fact that it was given by the great Washington to my tribal relative, Red Jacket, and that it was to be retained and worn as evidence of the bond of perpetual peace and friendship established and entered into between the people of the United States and the Six Nations of Indians at the time of its presentation.

Just how seriously Ely Parker took his new role can be seen by the letters he wrote from then on. No longer was he "E. S. Parker, Esq." The formal correspondence he sent to Albany, to Washington, and to anyone in an official capacity was signed:

E.S. Parker, Grand Sachem of the Six Nations of Indians in New York and Canada

In all fairness, though Ely claimed to be the primary representative of all the Iroquois people, often calling himself "head chief" or "principal sachem," that claim was not totally accurate. Iroquois sachems (royaners) were all of equal status, much like the senators in the United States government. Further, by 1851, part of the Seneca Nation—those living on the Cattaraugus Reservation—had formally broken away from the Six Nations and formed their own independent government. However, there is no doubt that most of the Tonawandas regarded him as their main spokesman—as well as many of those in other of the Six Nations whose causes Ely would champion—at their request—in the decades to come.

So, too, did the state of New York. In January 1853, Governor Horatio Seymour, in a formal statement, recognized "Grand Chief E. S. Parker, Do-ne-ho-ga-wa," as the "Elected Chief and Representative of the ancient confederacy of the Six Nations."

11

A VICTORY
AT LAST

They do not want it. They do not ask for it, nor would they take it even if it were left at their door, so strong is their determination not to barter away their rights and the true interests of their offspring.

—FROM ELY S. PARKER'S "NOTES
ON THE ROAD," JANUARY 1848

Almost exactly one month after being elevated to his new office in the Six Nations, on October 16, 1851, Ely S. Parker was appointed first assistant engineer on the state canals.

Ely's stature in both the white and Indian worlds had been greatly elevated. As a first assistant engineer, his prestige and financial rewards were greater. He could expect to enjoy his life in white society at a new level, accepted and respected as few Indians had ever been. His membership in the local atheneum, an organization formed to "advance the cultural life" of the city, afforded him access to their sizable library and reading room. Such famous speakers as Ralph Waldo Emerson and Frederick Douglass (who lived nearby) delivered lectures at the city's Corinthian Hall.

He was also rapidly progressing in the Rochester Mason's lodge and was one of their most popular public speakers. Having been advanced to the rank of a Knight Templar, he cut quite a figure when he stood before the crowd dressed in the uniform of a knight, including gauntlets and a sword!

Ely also was an active member of one of the city's military companies. In the mid-nineteenth century, in those years before the American Civil War, the United States government encouraged the formation of citizen militias as a way to reduce the regular army and make the armed forces "more compatible with our republican institutions." It also cut the country's costs for maintaining a large paid military. The Mexican–American War from 1845 to 1848—in which

MASONIC FLAG

President Franklin Pierce served as an officer—had employed almost 74,000 American soldiers. A good many of the former officers who had taken part in that conflict—which ended with a total U.S. victory and the annexation of much of the northern part of Mexico—found themselves out of work when it ended. Most of them continued voluntary military work in militias like the one Ely joined.

Ironically, though there had been victory against Mexico, one of the results of that conflict, General Ulysses S. Grant believed, was the American Civil War. "The Southern rebellion," Grant wrote in his memoirs, "was largely the outgrowth of the Mexican war." Whether that is true or not, one fact about that "easy" Mexican conflict is that it trained a large number of the men who served on either side in the art of war. Among those who later joined the side of the Confederate states were Stonewall Jackson, Robert E. Lee, and the future president of the Confederacy, Jefferson Davis.

Parker's own capabilities as an officer in Rochester's 54th Regiment appear to have been outstanding. Colonel Henry Fairchild, the regiment's commander, stated to Ely that "there is not an officer on my staff who has been more prompt nor one I think more of or respect higher than yourself."

Despite his success in the white world, Ely's Indian people still demanded his time and attention. As the new Grand Sachem, his responsibilities had been greatly increased. Not only was he a major representative of his Tonawanda Senecas, his position meant he carried a greater role for the entire confederacy. Now when he went to Albany, he might be speaking for any or all of the Six Nations.

Sadly, soon after Ely's investiture, his thirty-six-year-old brother, Spencer, who just had been installed as a war chief, became ill. And, in November 1851, he died.

Throughout that next year of 1852, despite the loss of a brother to whom he had become increasingly close, Ely continued to be highly visible as the major voice of the Iroquois Confederacy.

He also involved himself in national politics. In 1850, Millard Fillmore had succeeded to the land's highest office when Zachary Taylor died less than a year after being elected president. As a New York congressman, Fillmore had voiced support for one James Wadsworth of the Ogden Land Company, who had led an armed party of surveyors onto the reservation in 1848. Fillmore had even served as counsel for the Ogden Company. Further, before joining the Whigs, the new American president had originally belonged to another party—the Anti-Masons.

It was no surprise then that in the next election, Ely—both an Indian and a dedicated Mason—favored Franklin Pierce, the

Democratic candidate. In fact, in September 1852, Ely spoke at a Democratic rally in Fairport. Although an Indian, and therefore not a citizen and unable to cast a ballot, he declared that if he could vote, it would be for Pierce. When Pierce was elected, Ely could justifiably say that he had been a vocal supporter.

Meanwhile, aided by Ely's efforts on their behalf, the Senecas steadfastly resisted their removal. Seven years had passed since their removal had been decreed, but they were still there. In July 1853, Ely visited Washington to meet with George W. Manypenny, Pierce's new commissioner of Indian Affairs. Ely pointed out that his people were not "savages," to be sent west, but industrious and just as civilized as their white neighbors. Over the past three years the Tonawandas had built more than two dozen houses and barns, and two new schools had been established on the reservation. They were selling their surplus grain and livestock at local markets. (Ely, himself, had productive farmland on the reservation. Because of his work in Rochester it was left in the care of his brothers.) It seems that Ely's efforts to demonstrate the civilized nature of his people bore fruit. Two weeks later the Pierce administration had the agent who'd been appointed to pay the Indians for their land return those funds to the Ogden Land Company. However, despite the return of that money, the Ogden Company's claims to the Indian land still remained. Pierce's actions merely delayed the eviction of the Tonawandas. No final legal decision had been made. The Tonawandas were still in danger of losing their reservation.

Ely's stay in Rochester came to an end in 1855. Though it was widely felt that Ely was the logical choice for the position, another man was brought in to be the chief resident engineer. It was a political appointment and Ely's engineers voiced their disappointment, knowing the man chosen was much less qualified. Realizing that his own place as first assistant engineer was no longer secure and wanting to protect his loyal engineers from conflict and probably dismissal, Ely resigned his position.

He did so knowing that another job was waiting for him and his men. He had been offered the position as chief engineer for a project in Norfolk, Virginia. Taking his staff of engineers with him, Ely found himself in the American South for the first time. There, he was welcomed and respected as he oversaw the construction of the Chesapeake and Albemarle Ship Canal. Ironically, the next time he returned to Virginia less than a decade later, it would not be as a welcome guest.

Meanwhile, the Tonawandas steadfastly refused to give up the struggle to remain on their reservation. While there's no doubt that Ely's efforts were of vital importance, it's important to remember that the Tonawanda chiefs and clan mothers never gave up and that the cause of their small Native American community was supported by many people—most of them white—outside the reservation. Thousands of Americans signed petitions and wrote letters to their congressmen. In a fall 1856 visit to Washington, Ely and his brother Nic carried letters from such supporters. In one of those letters a resident of the nearby town of Batavia wrote that "nearly ninety-nine out of every one hundred of the inhabitants of this region" opposed the removal of the Indians to the west.

When Ely and Nic met President Pierce in person, they received a much more sympathetic response than from his predecessor, Fillmore. Pierce assured them that he would not, as Fillmore had done, appoint another agent who'd try to force the Indians to accept the Ogden Company's money. Instead, Pierce promised, he would allow things to be decided in the courts.

Pierce was as good as his word. In January 1857, the most important case involving the Tonawandas' right to remain on their reservation went to the Supreme Court: *Joseph Fellows v. Susan Blacksmith and Ely S. Parker*. Although he could never be a lawyer, the twenty-nine-year-old Ely now found himself before the highest court in the land. It was the case that arose from the Odgen Land Company's agents turning Chief Blacksmith out of his sawmill and assaulting him. John Martindale argued their case before the solemn justices, turning now and then to Ely for his input and suggestions.

On March 4, 1857, the decision of the judges was announced, even though Chief Justice Roger Taney was not present. He was preparing for another and more important decision—one involving a slave named Dred Scott—that was to be announced on March 6.

In the case of the Tonawandas versus the Ogden Land Company, the court refused to deal with the issue that the treaties that sold the Seneca lands in western New York were fraudulent. However, the court stated—quite clearly—that only the United States government had the right to remove the Tonawandas from their reservation and send them to their "new lands" in far-off Kansas. If anyone from the Ogden Land Company set foot on the reservation they would be breaking the law. Although it was not all Ely and Martindale might have hoped for, it was a victory. The Ogden Land Company was now powerless to remove them. As long as the federal government did not move to evict them, the Tonawandas could remain.

By all accounts, Ely was elated at their victory. It was, he and Martindale felt, nearly the final step in securing the Tonawanda lands for his people and their descendants. Their optimism proved to be well-founded. In November 1857, he and other men met with officials from the office of Indian Affairs, and negotiated and signed a new treaty. In return for giving up all rights to their lands in Kansas and the resettlement money promised them, they were allowed $256,000 for the purchase of their reservation lands that were "legally" owned by the Ogden Land Company.

John Martindale—who had devoted fifteen years to their cause—assisted them in the buying back of their homeland. In the end, they were able to secure only about 60 percent of the land that had been theirs before the treaty was signed. However, that land was now theirs by right of purchase and could never again be claimed by the Ogden Land Company.

Ely was justly proud of his accomplishment. In a letter dated September 10, 1860, to Benjamin Wilcox, his former principal at Yates Academy, he wrote:

Notwithstanding the President's order to remove the Indians, I succeeded in staying his heavy hand, entered into negotiations with him, by which I raised $300,000 and out of that sum I bought back for the Indians the homes in which they had always lived. They are now comfortably settled, fear nothing, owe nothing & have money in the bank. I am also relieved of a great responsibility, which was shouldered when yet a mere youth, the weight of which, I fear, has made me prematurely old.

A VICTORY AT LAST

To show their gratitude to Ely for his fourteen years of service in their cause, he was given an additional fifty acres by the Tonawandas to add to the family farm. Ely, though, was not spending much time now on the reservation. He was busy with his engineering career.

Meanwhile, that March 6 decision by the Supreme Court was reverberating throughout the nation. The court's 7–2 decision against Dred Scott, the African American slave who had attempted to sue for his freedom and that of his wife, was based in part on reasoning similar to that which denied Ely Parker the chance to be a lawyer. Slaves, like Indians, could not claim citizenship. Further, ruling in favor of Dred Scott's emancipation would "improperly deprive Scott's owner of his legal property."

It was a decision that deepened the tensions between the North and South and helped bring on the Civil War four years later, a conflict that would truly be life-changing for Ely Parker.

DRED SCOTT, PAINTING (DETAIL)
BY LOUIS SCHULZE, 1888

12

A GENTLEMAN, THO' AN INDIAN

(My visit home) almost made me weep to think my fate
had doomed me to walk in other channels. With such
feelings raging within me, after a few days I turned my
face westward, and made all possible haste to reach again
the scene of my labors, that I might drive such thoughts
far away from me.

—ELY PARKER LETTER TO M.B., DATED OCTOBER 2, 1859

By early 1857, the job of constructing the Chesapeake and
Albermarle Canal was well underway. Ely's own part in its
planning was complete. His eyes now were on an engineering
job with the federal government, something he felt his experience
and well-founded reputation as a superior engineer would help him
secure. He also could rely on his many connections in Albany and
Washington for recommendations.

Those connections and his qualifications served him well. The Treasury Department—which was in charge of federal engineering projects—gave him an appointment with the lighthouse office in Detroit, Michigan, as superintendent of lighthouse construction for the Upper Great Lakes. That appointment was short-lived. Soon after he arrived in Detroit on March 1, he received word that he was being given a new assignment—superintendent for the construction of a marine hospital and customhouse in Galena, Illinois, a job requiring him to do the work of both architect and engineer.

GALENA, ILLINOIS, LEVEE 1852–1854

When Ely arrived in Galena he discovered that his appointment had stirred a great deal of interest. The Democrats of Galena had not been informed of the decision to hire him. Senator Stephen Douglas of Illinois, whose nickname was "The Little Giant," was upset he'd not been consulted and complained to Howell Cobb, the Secretary of the Treasury, who had appointed Parker.

Cobb assured the diminutive but powerful senator (who would later run for the presidency against Lincoln) that Parker was well qualified. Without mentioning his appointee was an Indian, Cobb described Ely as "a Civil Engineer of known and tried capacity, who had been employed upon various public works in the state of New York & stood favourably before the late Secretary for his scientific attainments, integrity, and general fitness for the position."

Ely's first impression of Galena when he arrived on April 6, 1857, was not positive. In a letter written to his friend Lewis Blair that June, he described it as a "dark and benighted part of the globe" where hard drinking, fighting, and "the practice of cheating & bare faced lying" were the order of the day. There was also more open prejudice against Indians here on the western frontier, especially in Galena, which had been threatened with attack in the Black Hawk War only a little more than three decades before. Ely also discovered that the site chosen for the customhouse was on unstable ground, and that the stone needed to construct both it and the hospital could not be found locally. Further, federal government regulations required him to gain approval for even the smallest decisions.

However, if anyone was always up to a challenge, it was Ely. He communicated regularly and in great detail with the Treasury Department. He convinced the local authorities to choose a better site and was authorized to travel to quarries to find suitable stone. When he located the appropriate white limestone 240 miles down the Mississippi at Nauvoo, he opened a quarry—with the Treasury Department's approval—and shipped the stone north to Galena.

Despite his hard work and success, there was still resentment about his appointment. In June and July of 1857 he had to travel to Washington to plead the case of the Tonawandas to James Buchanan, the new president. When he returned to Galena he discovered that the Galena Democrats, still upset about not having had a voice in his hiring, and Senator Douglas were demanding his removal.

Ely, wanting to save his reputation, was ready to resign, rather than be discharged. But he had powerful friends in New York and Washington who endorsed him. So, too, did many people in Galena. Richard Jackson, a Galena lawyer, wrote letters protesting "the atrocious efforts of pot house politicians to remove Parker," praising him as "a gentleman, tho' an Indian." A petition on his behalf was signed by the mayor of Galena and the city aldermen. Finally, the Treasury Department, satisfied with his work, made no move to remove him and Ely was allowed to continue as superintendent.

Two years later, on August 8, 1859, the white limestone Galena customhouse was completed and formally inaugurated. It was built well. Still in use in the twenty-first century as the Galena Post Office building, it's said to be the longest operating such building in the United States. The *Galena Gazette* described the customhouse as "the most perfect structure north of St. Louis and west of Chicago"

GALENA CUSTOMHOUSE

and praised Ely, saying, "Mr. Parker has discharged the important duties of his important position to the satisfaction of everyone." Shortly after the customhouse, the handsome brick marine hospital was completed.

Ely developed strong ties in Galena during his two years there, especially among the Masons. He helped organize a new Masonic lodge, Miners Lodge No. 273, and was elected as its "first worshipful master." He also, despite being an Iroquois sachem pledged to always be a man of peace, was attracted to Galena's local militia companies. After all, his father had been an American soldier, and the idea of military service was familiar to him. In those years before the Civil War, civilian militias were the nineteenth-century equivalent of the twentieth-century peacetime National Guard. Most towns of any size prided themselves on their military organizations, and a great many of the most prominent men became civilian soldiers, often with no real expectation of ever going into combat. Ely joined a Galena militia, found he enjoyed military life, and rose to the rank of captain.

Although he moved in December 1858 to Dubuque, Iowa, to oversee the building of another, larger customhouse, it was only seventeen miles away. Thus it was not hard for him to return to Galena to maintain his contacts there.

13

TWO MILITARY MEN

My acquaintance with the general began in the summer
of 1860 at Galena, Illinois, where he was employed in his
father's store. I observed at our first meeting how very
diffident and reticent he was.

—E. S. PARKER, FROM *PERSONAL REFLECTIONS
OF THE WAR OF THE REBELLION*

I t was now 1860. Ely was living in a comfortable suite in the Julien
House, an elegant hotel in Dubuque. He was thirty-two years
old. It was an age at which men of his time had already married
and started families. But, though handsome and successful, by all
accounts Ely seemed to have had no interest in matrimony.

Why was this so? Part of the reason may have been that he was
too busy to seek a wife. His dual obligations were immense. He had

to represent the Indians of New York on one hand and carry out the task of his engineering responsibilities on the other. He and John Martindale were making frequent trips to Albany on behalf of the Tonawandas and other New York Native communities. In July 1860 alone, he traveled more than two thousand miles purchasing iron-work for the Dubuque customhouse.

There is also another reason, one that affected every aspect of Ely Parker's life all through his life. He was not white. His short-lived experience with a white girlfriend at Yates had taught him how he was viewed socially. To be an Indian was only one slight step up from being Black. In many censuses of the deeply racist nineteenth century (and well into the twentieth century), both Native Americans and African Americans were listed as "colored." Any white woman who gave serious thought to marrying an Indian might find herself an outcast.

So why did Ely not marry an Indian? For one, Ely was now largely living away from Tonawanda. His everyday life did not bring him into contact with Native women of marriageable age. Further, successful as he was, that success in the white world might not have seemed attractive to a Native woman committed to her own life and family ties. Remember, among the Iroquois, women have great power and status within their community. To make things even more complicated, one should never marry either a cousin or someone from the same clan. With a total population of only about seven hundred people at the time—many closely related to each other, the number of Tonawanda women culturally eligible for marriage had to have been extremely small. When Ely's sister, Carrie, married, it was not to a Seneca but to a Tuscarora.

And perhaps, too, as events later in his life would prove, Ely had just not met the right person.

Ely was truly an imposing presence, both mentally and physically. Despite his accomplishments, he remained modest and reticent to talk about himself, while still exhibiting the sense of humor that was so much a part of his character.

Two hundred pounds of encyclopedia was what one of his friends called him because it seemed he could talk intelligently about almost anything. He was five feet eight inches tall, which was above-average height for the mid-nineteenth century, and immensely strong. His shoulders were so broad that his coats had to be specially tailored.

His features were very much those of a northeastern Native American. His complexion was brown, his eyes dark and piercing, his thick hair jet-black and straight. He also was now sporting the mustache and goatee that he would keep for the rest of his life. Because Native Americans were so seldom imagined with facial hair, it sometimes led people to mistake him for a Middle Easterner, a South American, or an African American.

Though Ely was finding life in Dubuque comfortable, he did not develop friendships like those he'd found in Galena. It was in Galena that his Masonic lodge was located, as well as the military companies who knew him as Captain Parker. So, despite having his rooms in Dubuque, he seems to have spent at least as much time in Galena.

One of Ely's best friends, whom he met in Galena in 1858, was John E. Smith, a jeweler who belonged to Ely's Masonic lodge. It may be difficult for people today to understand just how strong such fraternal organization ties were in the nineteenth century. To be a brother Mason was close to being an actual brother.

Another good friend was a young lawyer named John Aaron Rawlins. Rawlins was a strong supporter of Stephen Douglas, the same senator who had been so hostile to Ely's appointment as an engineer. Somehow, Rawlins managed to win Ely over and by 1860 Ely was supporting Douglas in his bid for the presidency.

One day, while visiting a dry-goods store in Galena, he noticed a rather unusual person he'd never seen before working there. Ely wryly observed that:

> Selling goods from behind a counter did not seem to be his forte, for if he was near the front door when a customer entered, he did not hesitate to make a pretty rapid retreat to the counting-room which was in the rear part of the building, leaving the visitor to be waited on by some other employee.

Somehow, Ely managed to engage the man in conversation. It turned out they had much in common. Both were trained engineers, though Ely's training had been in the field and not the classrooms of West Point. Both were military men, though Ely's captaincy had merely been with a local militia rather than while serving in the Mexican–American War. They even shared an acquaintance with the former president Franklin Pierce, though Ely's had been during conversations in the White House rather than playing cards in Mexico City.

The man's diffidence and reticence, which hid "a warm and sympathetic nature," reminded Ely "a great deal of some of my Indian friends." A deep relationship developed as Ely "saw him frequently, becoming friendly by degrees as we became better acquainted, which friendship continued to the day of his death."

One thing about Ely that stands out throughout his life is the way he seems to have been liked and respected by his friends. It would certainly prove to be so with that reticent young clerk who had been forced to work in his father's store when the United States Army was downsized after the Mexican war. Ulysses S. Grant would not forget Ely Parker.

14

AN
OFFER
TO SERVE

Mr. Seward in a short time said to me that the struggle in which I wished to assist, was an affair between white men and one in which the Indian was not called on to act.

—LETTER FROM ELY S. PARKER,
SEPTEMBER 3, 1861

The year 1860 was a crucial one in the life of the American nation. The great debate over the right of the southern states to maintain the institution of slavery was becoming more and more heated. Compromise after compromise had been attempted, but the two sides were further apart than ever before. The question of whether the new territories won in the Mexican war would be "Slave States" or "Free States"; John Brown's raid on Harpers Ferry, which had been meant to create a slave revolt; the Dred Scott decision; and the publication of the novel *Uncle Tom's Cabin*, which dramatized the inhuman nature of slavery, contributed to stirring things up to a simmer. The election of 1860 would cause that pot to boil over.

The year also marked another turning point in the life of Ely Parker, one that seemed to echo the image in his mother's dream of a rainbow broken at its highest point. Ironically, that break would be at least partially a result of Ely's public support of Stephen Douglas, who ran against Abraham Lincoln. With his usual oratorical strength, Ely had made speeches for Douglas at Democratic rallies in New York State during the presidential campaign.

When Abraham Lincoln won, the usual scramble for places in the new administration began. Democrats were out and Republicans were in. Political appointees like Ely Parker, men who had chosen the wrong side, found themselves being replaced by Lincoln men. William Martin, a Dubuque brick mason put together a petition asking that Parker be dismissed. Martin also, taking advantage of the stereotype of Indians as drunks, sent reports to Washington accusing Ely of being intoxicated on the job. Salmon P. Chase, the new Secretary of the Treasury, ordered William Buell Franklin, the engineer in charge of Treasury Department construction, to remove the Indian.

Although Franklin defended Ely, staying that Parker was "never suspected of being a drinking man" and that he had "performed well and systematically," it did no good. On March 26, 1861, Ely was removed from his position and William Martin took his place. Although he was given a certificate of appreciation for his work, Ely realized what this meant. "I do not expect," he wrote in a letter dated April 8, 1861, "ever again to hold any public position." He tried to find private jobs in engineering. But despite months of trying, even with recommendations from his influential friends, no offers came his way. His career as an engineer was over.

ELY FIXED UP THIS HOUSE FOR HIS PARENTS IN TONAWANDA.

AN OFFER TO SERVE

By the summer of 1861, out of work and with no prospects of future employment, Ely Parker was back at his farm on the reservation. He was given the position of clerk of the Tonawanda Senecas, a position he had suggested the tribe needed due to their new circumstances. But little work was required there. In a letter to J. Russell Jones, one of his friends from Galena, he confided that he was making no profit from his farm—which cost more to run than a Mississippi steamboat. He'd thought about marriage, but found no prospects. "Do you know," he wrote to Jones, "among your extensive list of female acquaintances, a good, strong, healthy [woman] who would like to be a farmer's wife? If so, recommend me."

He also, in his ample spare time, turned again to Masonry. He organized a new Masonic lodge in Akron, near the reservation, and was elected in 1862 as its first master.

The drumbeat of war was being heard everywhere in the land by then. Fort Sumter had fallen to the Confederacy on April 13, 1861. Abraham Lincoln had sent out an impassioned call for volunteers.

Before returning to Tonawanda, Ely had visited Galena. He found his friends preparing for war. John Rawlins said he would stand by the flag, despite the fact he was a Democrat, and volunteer to serve. John E. Smith, the Galena jeweler and fellow Mason, was

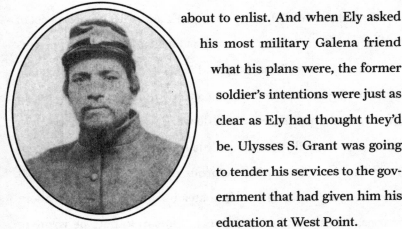

JACOB WINNIE WAS ONE OF MANY
SENECA SOLDIERS WHO SERVED
IN THE UNION ARMY.

about to enlist. And when Ely asked his most military Galena friend what his plans were, the former soldier's intentions were just as clear as Ely had thought they'd be. Ulysses S. Grant was going to tender his services to the government that had given him his education at West Point.

Back on the Tonawanda Reservation, the war was the main topic of conversation. As had been the case in every war since the American Revolution, Iroquois men were ready to defend their homeland by serving in the United States military. Ely went to his father—the proper Seneca way to do things, even though Ely was thirty-two years old—to ask his permission to enlist. That permission was granted—though his war-wounded father worried about his son now going into battle. Ely then went to Albany. There, he asked Governor Edwin D. Morgan for a commission. Ely's idea was, as a militia captain, to put together his own engineering company as a commanding officer. Qualified engineers were among those greatly needed by the Union Army. However, no commission was given to him. Whether it was because he was an Indian or because Morgan was chairman of the Republican National Committee is not known. Morgan, himself, would leave office as governor in 1862 to serve—with distinction—as a Union general.

Ely Parker was never one to give up easily. His friend John Martindale, the lawyer who did so much to assist the Tonawanda struggle for their land, was now a brigadier general. In September, Ely visited him where he was stationed near Washington. It may have been Martindale who suggested Ely's next move. William H. Seward, a fellow New Yorker who had spoken in the Senate on behalf of the Indians, was now the secretary of state. It was to Seward that Ely went to offer his service. But he was rebuffed yet again. Seward stated firmly that there was no place for him in the Grand Army of the Republic. The fight must be made and settled by white men alone. "Go home," Seward told him, "cultivate your farm, and we will settle our own troubles among ourselves without any Indian aid."

Tenacious as ever, Ely tried another approach. The fact that Indians were not citizens was one reason for denying his service. He used his expertise from years of negotiation to prepare a petition asking that he be granted citizenship. He then submitted it to Congress. The petitioner, he stated:

... is a freeholder, paying taxes in the states of New York, Iowa and Minnesota [who] has held various positions of trust and honor in the state and federal service, and that he has a high veneration for the laws of this, his native country, and he respectfully prays your Honorable Body to grant him the rights, privileges, and franchises of an American citizen.

Ely's petition made its way to the House Judiciary Committee, which considered the matter—but stated that the uniform rules of citizenship did not include the power to confer it on a single Indian.

Disappointed, Ely returned home. There, he began serving as elected clerk of the Tonawanda Senecas and represented his people on trips to Albany. However, this life and the occupation of farming gave him no satisfaction. "While my hands labor . . . plodding after the plow," he wrote to J. Russell Jones, "my mind loafs away to other scenes."

In 1862, his mother died on February 23 at the age of seventy-five after a short illness. Dressed in the traditional regalia of an honored matriarch, she was laid to rest on the land her son had helped save for the coming generations. The grief of her husband—himself in ill health—and their children was deep. "This sad and awful bereavement," Ely wrote to his brother Nic, "throws a great gloom upon our family."

Meanwhile, the war was dragging on. Thoughts in the North of a quick victory vanished. Though outgunned and outnumbered, the Southern side was blessed with effective and brilliant commanders. Chief among them was General Robert E. Lee. Lee had served with great distinction in the Mexican–American War. He'd also been the commander of the U.S. forces that put down John Brown's Raid on the United States' arsenal in Harpers Ferry in 1859.

At the start of the Civil War, Lincoln had offered command of the Union Army to Lee, whose stately home, the Custis-Lee Mansion, was across the Potomac from the nation's capital. Lee declined the offer. He did not want to see the Union dissolved, but he could never take arms against his native state of Virginia. Soon Lee was in charge of the Confederate military and was proving himself superior to the Union generals.

By mid-1862, the Union Army was in deep need of new recruits. Some Indians from other tribes had already been allowed to enlist. Colonel John Fisk approached Ely. Fisk hoped to add two or three companies of Indians to the regiment he was raising in western New York. Fisk, perhaps ignorant of the fact that sachems traditionally could not go to war, believed that Ely Parker, as Grand Sachem, could help him bring in at least three hundred Senecas—and then lead them into battle.

Ely did help raise those recruits for the 53rd Regiment of New York volunteers. His brother Nic was enlisted as third sergeant in Company D. But for some reason, that offer of command to the Grand Sachem was not honored. Was it because Ely had been so strongly identified as a "Douglas man"? For whatever reason, the 53rd left New York without Ely.

Ely must have been deeply discouraged by then. Nearly two years had passed since he first tried to enlist. It seemed that Seward's discouraging words had come true—at least for him, since other Iroquois were already in the Union Army. All he could do now was stay home and cultivate his farm. But his white friends already serving had not forgotten him.

15

AS
MUCH
UNDER FIRE

I was at Vicksburg with the chivalric and lamented McPherson. I was with Grant at Chattanooga, in the Wilderness, at Spotsylvania, Cold Harbor, Petersburg and at Appomattox where the rebellion closed its haggard eyes in death never to open them again.

—FROM GENERAL ELY S. PARKER'S
AUTOBIOGRAPHY

The same John E. Smith who had been one of Ely's closest companions in Illinois was now a brigadier general. Smith was well aware of his Indian friend's reliability, his administrative and engineering qualifications. He also knew, as did all of Ely's friends now serving in high-ranking positions, how desperately Ely wished to serve.

On April 2, 1863, Smith wrote to Washington. He requested that one Ely S. Parker, a man well qualified by education and experience, a "good practical Civil Engineer," be appointed to his staff as an assistant adjutant general. General Grant himself endorsed the request, following up with a letter of his own.

On May 25, Ely's commission was issued. A courier carrying the commission, which "bore the great red seal of the War Department," found Ely and presented it to him. But he did not formally accept it until June 4. As Grand Sachem, one of the fifty, he was not supposed to be a warrior. It had always been the responsibility of the clan mothers to choose whether or not their nation would go to war. So he went to the eight Tonawanda clan mothers to see if he might gain their permission. Their decision was quickly made. This was a "white man's war" and not against another Indian tribe. Thus, Donehogawa could retain his sachemship and accept the commission as an assistant adjutant general in the Union army.

It was an appropriate role for one as well educated and used to dealing with a large staff as Ely had been as a head engineer. An adjutant general officer is one who is responsible for providing personnel support, accounting for the well-being of his soldiers and keeping them combat ready. It is more of an "indoor" job than one out in the field.

Packing his belongings, including the Red Jacket medal, Ely made ready to depart for Mississippi to join Smith's division. A crowd of six hundred Senecas had gathered when he rode up on his fine black horse to bid them farewell and take part in a feast put on in his honor where he would receive the blessing of the elders. According to the recollection of his niece, someone in that crowd of Tonawandas called out, "Who will be our friend if you are killed?"

Ely must have smiled at that. "I am determined to go," he replied. "I am sure that I will be all right."

Traveling by way of Cincinnati, Ohio, and Cairo, Illinois, where he boarded a steamboat, he arrived in Memphis, Tennessee, on July 2, 1863. It was there he learned that the armies of General Grant had defeated the forces of Confederate General Pemberton and taken Vicksburg. When Ely reached Smith's headquarters five days later, one of the first people he saw was his old friend from Galena.

My commanding general and myself called upon General Grant, by whom we were kindly and graciously entertained for over an hour. The General was in excellent humor, and well he might be, after having taken this place and broken one of the best appointed armies of the Confederate States.

Over the next several days, the new army officer was able to watch the defeated men of Pemberton's army being marched out of town, so many that it took them two full days to leave. They were, he said in a letter to his friend H. J. Ensign, "a hard-looking set of men" who might make "splendid soldiers for the Evil One himself." Ely also observed that the entire country within the rebel works was "one vast cemetery" with "the dead buried very carelessly, for we frequently see the head or some of the limbs protruding out of the ground." With quite literal graveyard humor he added that "My horse stepped on a poor fellow's stomach, putting his foot clear through him. It did not, of course, hurt him, but it was very disagreeable to me."

Ely had been commissioned as an assistant adjutant general. However, Smith's 7th Division was lacking an engineer. As the man best suited to that position, Ely was assigned as division engineer. However, the 7th Division of the 17th Army Corps remained in camp at Vicksburg for the rest of the summer. As a result, Ely's duties as an engineer were few until the new orders for the division arrived in September. They were to advance to Little Rock, Arkansas, to reinforce General Frederick Steele in taking the city.

About to head into combat at last, Ely drew up his will.

Should he be killed, his property was to be divided equally between his father and Ely's favorite siblings—his sister, Carrie, and his brother Nic. However, soon after the division set out, word came that Little Rock had fallen and they were ordered to make camp on the Mississippi flats near the town of Helena.

Ely himself did not stay there long. On September 18, he was given a new assignment. He was named as assistant adjutant general on General Grant's personal staff.

Ely was just the man Grant needed. Ely's old friend's staff was lacking the kind of competence the well-educated Seneca could bring. It was a curious mixture of the good, bad, and indifferent, "a mosaic of accidental elements and family friends," as Charles Dana, the assistant secretary of war, described Grant's staff. A few West Point graduates and their mutual friend from Galena, John Rawlins, were among the good, but they were in the minority. And none of Grant's staff could write the English language well. Ely Parker's training in engineering and in the law, and above all, his ability to write grammatically, thus made him an invaluable asset. Plus, unlike many other military secretaries, his penmanship was perfect. Before long he was writing—and helping compose—all of Grant's orders.

GENERAL ULYSSES GRANT AND STAFF. ELY IS SEATED SECOND FROM THE RIGHT. PHOTOGRAPH BY MATHEW BRADY, CIRCA 1864.

Modest and capable, Ely Parker, the Indian at army headquarters, soon found himself fully accepted. Life was not easy, though. A few days after his arrival, Ely came down with a case of the ague, the term used for malaria in the nineteenth century. It was so extreme the doctor attending him said he was probably going to die. Such illnesses were quite common in the South then, and often as many soldiers were casualties from sickness as fell on the battlefields. The medical treatment for ague was primitive. Part of Ely's treatment, prescribed by the army physician, was to have him consume sizable doses of alcohol. Ely lost thirty pounds, but survived. Whether or not the alcohol helped is uncertain. But what is certain is that, historically, alcohol has been devastating to Native Americans.

Handsome Lake, the Seneca prophet, had himself fallen into a coma after drinking too much and nearly died from alcohol poisoning. In his Good Message he stated clearly the terrible problem of drinking.

Ely was familiar with his famous ancestor's warning words. Despite their Baptist upbringing—which also emphasized temperance—the teachings of Handsome Lake were part of the Parker household. But, although he was aware of the dangers of consuming large amounts of alcohol, there's no doubt that Ely engaged in social drinking while serving with Grant and during the years after the war in Washington. There were attempts in Galena and Dubuque—and even later in his career—to paint Ely as a drunken Indian. But it appears his detractors did so to block the advance of an Indian seeking a white man's place in a racist world. There seems to have been little or no truth to the image of Ely Parker as a problem drinker. What drinking he did never impaired his ability to do his job before, during, or after the Civil War.

Later in life, in fact, according to his grand-nephew and biographer Arthur C. Parker, Ely completely swore off alcohol. At one point, "after a severe illness his physician told him to take a dram of whiskey at certain intervals." Ely said no, even when he was told, "You must use it or you may die." Ely absolutely refused and lived—without drinking.

Though still weak from the ague, in January 1864, Ely traveled with Grant to the army's new military headquarters in Chattanooga.

During the five-day battle for Missionary Ridge on January 17, Ely was by Grant's side "as much under fire as the Genl himself." The following description that Parker wrote of Grant in battle appeared in the *New York Times*:

> It has been a matter of universal wonder in this army that General Grant himself was not killed, and that no more accidents occurred to his staff for the General was always in the front (his staff with him, of course), and perfectly heedless of the storm of hissing bullets and screaming shell flying around him. His apparent want of sensibility does not arise from heedlessness, heartlessness, or vain military affectation, but from a sense of responsibility resting upon him when in battle. When at Ringgold, we rode for half a mile in the face of the enemy, under an incessant fire of cannon and musketry—nor did we ride fast, but at an ordinary trot, and not once do I believe did it enter the general's mind that he was in danger. I was by his side and watched him closely.

When that battle was over and Grant decided to issue a congratulatory order to his troops, he turned to Ely to write it for him. And though Grant sent it out under his own name, the structure and virtually every word of the eloquently phrased order came from the pen of Ely Parker.

You dislodged him from his great stronghold upon Lookout Mountain, drove him from Chattanooga Valley, wrested from his determined grasp the possession of Missionary Ridge, repelled with heavy loss his repeated assaults upon Knoxville, forcing him to raise the siege there, driving him at all points, utterly routed and discomfited, beyond the limits of the State.

Their headquarters then moved to Nashville. Ely had the opportunity to see the Hermitage, the home of Andrew Jackson, not far from the city. Although the removal of all of the Indians of the East and Southeast was one of President Jackson's pet projects, Ely seemed not to have dwelled on that, merely describing his excursion as a pleasant visit.

He also had time to play frequent games of billiards with a new friend, Samuel Beckwith, who was the man in charge of the army cipher. Beckwith, like virtually everyone who came into contact with Ely, was impressed by the Indian soldier's quiet competence,

saying that he was "never disturbed, excited or hurried by passing events," and that "his silent desk yielded its regular quota of handsomely written sheets at the proper moment."

Ely Parker was now well-known to everyone in Grant's army as "The Indian." Whether working at his desk or riding on his spirited large black horse, he was always close to the general.

When, in March, President Lincoln gave Grant command of the forces in Virginia, Ely was among those few members of his staff chosen by the general to accompany him. First, however, Ely made a brief visit to Tonawanda to see his father, who was gravely ill. It was the last time he would see him. Shortly after arriving at Grant's headquarters in Culpeper Courthouse, his sister, Carrie, telegraphed him. Their father had walked on.

With both parents gone, Ely felt his last real ties to the reservation had been severed. He might visit there, but it would never be his home again.

He confided as much to his friend and former commanding officer General John E. Smith. He was, Ely said, "now afloat and without an anchor in this wide world."

ELY PARKER IN UNION UNIFORM, 1867

16

WE ARE ALL AMERICANS

This life, though dangerous, suits me charmingly. At times I have been exposed to the death-dealing missiles thrown at us by the enemy, thus far, however, thanks to a Great over-ruling Spirit, I am unharmed.

—ELY PARKER TO "MY DEAR FRIEND," JUNE 8, 1864

Ely Parker was not the only Indian or even the only Seneca who fought in the Civil War. His younger brother Isaac Newton Parker successfully enlisted in 1862 and served in a company largely made up of Tuscaroras. Unlike his famous older brother, he was a common foot soldier, eventually gaining the rank of sergeant as his company saw action in North Carolina. When the war ended in 1865 he was offered a military commission in the regular army but chose instead to go west as a teacher.

In the South, many of the North Carolina Cherokees—who had avoided being sent west on the Trail of Tears—chose to enlist in the army. And in the West, in Indian Territory, the Cherokee Nation was divided against itself. Many Cherokees chose to join the southern cause, led by Stand Watie. Watie's grievances against the Cherokee government led by John Ross stemmed from the events decades before when Watie's friends and relatives, who'd signed the treaty agreeing to the Cherokee removal, had been assassinated. Watie held the full rank of general and was the last Confederate general to surrender when the war ended.

That feeling was understandable considering what was happening to other Native Americans in the West during the period of the Civil War. In August 1862, the Minnesota Dakotas (also known as the Sioux) rose up, attacking settlers. One main cause of the uprising was the government's failure to provide promised

DEGATAGA. CHEROKEE CHIEF STAND WATIE.

rations and that the murders of Dakotas by settlers went unpunished. Hundreds died in the Sioux Wars that ended in December when thirty-eight Dakota men were executed in Mankato. It was the largest mass hanging in American history. The entire Dakota Nation, as well as the Ho-Chunk Nation (who had no part in the uprising) were expelled from Minnesota, their reservations abolished.

In 1864, in Arizona, a scorched-earth campaign was begun against the Navajo people. They were told to either surrender or be destroyed. U.S. soldiers under the command of Kit Carson systematically burned crops and villages and slaughtered Navajo livestock. Thousands of Navajos surrendered. They were then forced to walk three hundred miles across the desert to a barren place called the Bosque Redondo in New Mexico, where the soil was too dry and salty to grow crops. Many of the eight thousand or more Navajos died along the way.

On November 29, 1864, a 675-man force of U.S. Volunteer Cavalry attacked a peaceful Cheyenne and Arapaho village near Sand Creek in Colorado. Led by a brutal officer named Colonel John Chivington, they killed and mutilated the bodies of as many as five hundred Native Americans—two-thirds of them women and children.

Considering those events, which were similar to the way the Five Civilized Tribes of the South (Cherokee, Choctaw, Chickasaw, Creek, and Seminole) were treated early in the nineteenth century, it is little wonder that General Watie and other Cherokees felt that the Confederate government might be fairer to the Indian.

Ironically, despite being a Native American, Ely was one who believed in the right of the United States to control the continent. On more than one occasion before the Civil War he had seriously considered going west himself, perhaps settling in Oregon. Although he certainly knew of the Minnesota Dakota uprising, the tragic Navajo Long Walk, and the massacre at Sand Creek, it did not lessen his desire to serve the larger American nation, whose destiny he saw linked to his own.

Ely Parker's service did not start until the Civil War was entering its third year. However, he arrived at what would prove to be its turning point. Until Ulysses S. Grant was given control of the army, a variety of generals had held the position. President Lincoln had complained about their timidity and lack of decisiveness. None of them had the stubbornness or the staying power of Grant. As Grant's secretary, Ely would experience firsthand the Virginia Campaign that would lead to the South's eventual surrender.

He would also bear witness to the sort of man Grant showed himself to be.

> Grant never cared much about how he looked, but he did take care of his hat while riding. If a twig hit it and made a dent he would take it off and smooth it out. I think General Grant was a little proud of his riding. He would gallop off to meet some officer and dashing up would suddenly rein his horse and dismount before the horse had stopped.

Although Ely was not a front-line soldier, he did find himself exposed to danger. While riding beside his friend Rawlins, a rebel cannon farther up the road was fired at them. Ely actually saw the cannon ball coming straight at him. It would have hit him, but he swung to the side and the cannon ball merely brushed his sleeve.

On one notable occasion, Ely apparently saved Grant from capture or death. On May 4, 1864, Grant crossed the Rapidan River. The Battle of the Wilderness that followed was a desperate struggle. The woods and heavy brush caught fire and soldiers on both sides often lost their way. Night had fallen. General Grant and General George Gordon Meade—who had defeated Lee at Gettysburg—were on their way to their headquarters at a place called Todd's Tavern. The smoke from the burning woods was everywhere and the road ahead of them clogged with wagons.

Colonel Cyrus Comstock, Grant's aide-de-camp, suggested they try a road that led off to the right. Riding close behind the generals, Ely realized that something was wrong.

The years of training Ely had spent at Grand River had never left him. Even in an unfamiliar setting he could find his way through the woodlands that night in the Wilderness. As Ely himself put it years later, "I developed the instinct to feel the presence of game or danger. Perhaps I had the good will of the spirits."

On that day he sensed that the direction they were heading would lead them into danger. "If he doesn't look out," Ely told Rawlins, who was riding beside him, "he will be in the rebel lines." Rawlins immediately called out to General Grant.

"Hey! General! Do you know where you are?"

Grant stopped his horse. "No," he said. He looked to the man leading them. "Comstock," Grant asked. "Do you?"

"No," answered Comstock.

Ely and Rawlins had by now ridden up to Grant's side.

"Parker says if you don't look out we will ride plumb into the rebel lines," Rawlins said.

Grant turned to Ely. "Parker," he said, "do you know where we are?"

"Yes, General," Ely replied.

Then, as Ely put it:

"Grant then quickly said, 'Well, then lead.' I put spurs to my black horse and galloped off in another direction and they full tilt after me."

Ely's intuition proved to have been right.

After the battle I met a rebel captain whom we had captured and he said to me, "Colonel, I wish to ask you about a certain incident. The other day I saw General Grant with General Meade and a party of which you were one riding into our lines. My men wanted to fire on you, but I said, 'Hold on, they will ride in and we can capture the whole lot.' Then I saw you ride up and say something to Grant and then your whole party galloped off in haste. You were within forty rods of us and we hoped to get you all in the next five minutes.

In addition to serving as Grant's secretary, and at times his watchdog, Ely often found himself engaging in engineering. Helping set up batteries or artillery, making sure that breastworks were properly built, and various other tasks were part of his routine.

J. T. Lockwood, who served with the 4th New York Heavy Artillery, described Colonel Parker's role on May 4 at Mechanicsville near Richmond. They had just asked the women of the Shelton house, a large southern home, to leave because the Union troops were setting up artillery nearby and the house might come under fire. The women haughtily refused to do as they were asked.

> "We shall not leave this house for my husband is in command of the troops over there and there is no danger of this house being fired upon."
>
> Colonel Parker then said politely, "Stay as long as you please, ladies, we shall not harm you." Then, turning to his officers, he roared, "Throw up a redoubt directly back of this house and plant a battery there."
>
> It was a clever bit of strategy for that battery did unmerciful work and it was a long time before the rebels sent a shell in our direction.

By the winter of 1864 and 1865, Grant was well settled in his headquarters at City Point. His tent was far from luxurious. It was little different—aside from its size—from the quarters of lesser officers. The furniture was rough wooden benches, and Grant slept on a simple army cot. A fire was kept burning outside, and Grant, with Ely close by, could usually be found there with his officers or sharing meals at a common table.

The war had reached the crisis point. The southern forces were now suffering one defeat after another. A final northern victory in 1865 seemed likely. There were rumors of spies in the camp and of plots to assassinate Grant. Ely often placed himself outside the door of Grant's tent, revolver in hand, as guard.

When President Lincoln came to visit, he shared meals at that same table with Grant and his officers, including Ely, of course. At one point, Lincoln spent a full two weeks at City Point. During his visit, Lincoln and Ely sat together several times in quiet conversation. During those talks, as Arthur C. Parker put it, his great-uncle "outlined his plans for the betterment of conditions, and pleaded for the education of the young. Lincoln was most sympathetic and said that he knew the Indians had suffered awful injustice which he hoped the nation some day would requite."

By March 1865, the great armies of the North and the South were facing each other along the Appomattox. Grant's plan was a simple one. He would drive forward and force Lee from his fortifications. He would trap Lee on all sides. He called in General Philip Sheridan to order him and his cavalry to harass the Confederates from the rear, force the enemy out to attack.

Headquarters, Armies of the United States

City Point, VA., March 29, 1865

Special Orders

No. 64

May. Gen. P.H. Sheridan, commanding Middle Military Division will order the detachment of Company D Fifth U.S. Cavalry, now serving with him to report immediately to these headquarters, wherever they may be, in the field.

By command of Lieutenant General U.S. Grant.

E.S. Parker

Acting Assistant Adjutant General

Grant's strategy worked. By the end of the month, Sheridan held the strategic position of Five Forks. Lee's Army of Northern Virginia resisted, but with the Union Army pressing forward, he had to retreat. On April 2, Petersburg fell, and on April 3, Grant's army took Richmond, the capital of the Confederate States.

Lee's army, reduced to fifty thousand troops, was fleeing. Battle after battle had been lost. Sheridan's cavalry had cut Lee's supply lines and the rebel troops were in a starving condition. Lee, though, stubbornly refused to surrender.

On April 7, Grant dictated to Ely this message that was sent to the southern leader.

GENERAL:—The results of the last week must convince you of the hopelessness of further resistance on the part of the Army of Northern Virginia in this struggle. I feel that it is so, and regard it as my duty to shift from myself the responsibility of any further effusion of blood, by asking of you the surrender of that portion of the Confederate States' army known as the Army of Northern Virginia.

U.S. Grant, Lieutenant General

Lee refused to surrender, but his cause was lost. Although he thought there was open country ahead of him to cross and join forces with another Confederate force, Sheridan's cavalry cut off his line of retreat. When Lee attacked Sheridan's forces, another Union force, commanded by General Edward Ord, closed in. Lee was trapped. Rather than make one final, desperate charge, he sent forward a white flag.

On Sunday, April 9, 1865, a note from General Lee was received by Grant as he and his staff were on their way to see Sheridan.

Grant dictated a reply to Lee's note. General Orville Babcock, who was also one of his secretaries, delivered Grant's response to Lee, who was found resting under an apple tree. (And then the events described in chapter 1 took place.)

The war was essentially drawing to a close with Lee's formal surrender. As good as that news of Lee's surrender was for the men of the Union Army, it was not good at all for the innocent tree that had sheltered Lee under its boughs.

"That apple tree," Ely would write, "was taken up by the roots and cut up into charms and other ornaments. I have one on my watch-chain."

Another souvenir that Ely collected from that momentous occasion was one of the three yellow manifold copies of the terms of surrender as he wrote them out before rewriting the terms in ink. Ely put it into his pocket and kept it all of his life.

As the meeting ended, other items began vanishing from the McLean parlor, grabbed by army officers as keepsakes. Among those who took part in that nostalgic larceny was none other than Brevet General George Armstrong Custer, who emerged with a small writing table.

On the next morning, April 10, Grant and his staff rode out to meet with Lee. They sat on their horses on a hill overlooking the Confederate camps, quietly talking. Of Grant's officers, only Ely Parker remained by his side during that meeting, helping take down the terms of surrender.

That same afternoon, Grant and members of his staff, including Ely, boarded the steamer *Mary Martin* at City Point to return to

UNION HEADQUARTERS, CITY POINT, VIRGINIA. ELY IS IN FRONT ROW, SECOND FROM RIGHT.

Washington. They arrived in the nation's capital on April 13, where Grant started making arrangements to end the draft and reduce the immense wartime expenditures. He was also invited to the White House and met with President Lincoln.

The next day, April 14, was Good Friday. Ely, too, received an invitation to meet with Lincoln, who wanted to renew his acquaintance with the interesting, well-spoken Indian officer he'd enjoyed his time with at City Point. Their meeting was a pleasant one. It afforded Ely the opportunity to do as he always did on momentous occasions—display the Red Jacket medal. Apparently Lincoln was suitably impressed when Ely—as he put it—"spoke feelingly of the associations it represented." It's possible that Lincoln suggested Ely might wish to extend his time with the president. An amusing play called *Our American Cousin* was being performed that night at Ford's Theatre. Just the sort of thing to take the president's mind off the heavy responsibilities of healing a wounded nation that lay ahead. But Ely was to go to New York on leave later that day. The two—the tall lanky president, whose weary years at war were finally over, and the burly, brilliant Seneca soldier—could meet and deepen their ties of friendship at a later date. So they must have hoped.

Ely did not return to Washington until late May. The Grand Review of the Union Army was taking place. Two days of celebration filled the capital's streets. Troops marched past the reviewing stand in front of the White House, where the new president, Andrew Johnson, and his cabinet watched. Newspapers described how thunderous applause greeted the arrival—on foot—of General Ulysses S. Grant and a few of his staff. By Grant's side, like a watchful shadow, was "Grant's favored aid . . . a huge colonel, dusky-faced." Ely, of course. When asked by a reporter about his feelings on Lincoln's assassination, his response was a direct and impassioned one: "You white men are Christians, and may forgive the murder. I am of a race which never forgets the murder of a friend."

ULYSSES GRANT AND STAFF IN BOSTON, 1865. ELY IS AT LEFT.

INDIAN AFFAIRS

It is a fact not to be denied that at this day Indian trading licenses are much sought after, and when once obtained, although it may be for a limited period, the lucky possessor is considered as having already made his fortune.

—FROM ELY PARKER'S
FOUR-POINT PROPOSAL

Although Andrew Johnson was the new president, no one was more popular in the years immediately following the Civil War than General Ulysses S. Grant. He toured the nation, accompanied by a few of his staff, always including Ely. An army of autograph seekers greeted them everywhere they went, and Ely's signature was nearly as often requested as the general's.

In September 1865 a commission was sent to Fort Smith,

Arkansas, to deal with twelve of the western tribes who'd allied with the Confederacy. President Johnson appointed Ely to be one of the commissioners at the recommendation of the secretary of war. His role turned out to be a very active one, presiding over the council and addressing the tribes for the commission. A successful agreement was reached in which the tribes pledged their loyalty to the United States. When Ely returned in October, he and Grant visited the White House to meet with Johnson and his cabinet, who were "very well pleased with the success of our mission west."

Ely's official position was as a member of Grant's military staff. He was also, alongside his friend Bowers, acting as one of Grant's secretaries. But his time was not just being spent at a desk. Now that the war was over, the army was being downsized. In January 1866, he was called on to make an inspection tour of the main southern military posts in Kentucky, Mississippi, and Tennessee to consider what units could be mustered out, what buildings and supplies sold.

The conditions of the former slaves there convinced him that keeping troops in the South was "an absolute necessity." Although now free, they still remained vulnerable and at the mercy of the whites around them—many of whom were "unreconstructed." In his report to the federal government, Ely said that:

To guard against an unjust oppression of the negro, to prevent personal conflicts between the two races, and to see that equal and just laws are enacted and executed seems to be the combined duty of the Freedman's Bureau and the military in the South, and until these things are accomplished it seems pretty clear that both of these institutions must be maintained in the South.

Ely was also being constantly called upon by the Indian Office for his assistance in dealing with delegations from Indian country, as well as affairs relating to the Tonawandas. "Hardly any thing affecting the New York Indians," Ely wrote to his brother Nic, "is acted upon without my being first consulted about it & what I say determines the matter."

Indian affairs in general were now a main concern of the nation. For the remainder of the nineteenth century, conflicts with the western tribes would be the main focus of the American military. At Grant's request, Ely began work on a plan that might—as he put it—establish "a permanent and perpetual peace . . . between the United States and the various Indian tribes."

His plan, submitted in January 1867, had four points:

First, Indian Affairs, then under the control of the Department of the Interior, should be returned to the War Department. Only the

ELY IN 1863

military could adequately protect the Indians whose treaty rights were being ignored and whose reservations were being disturbed by the tide of western settlers.

Second, the Indians should be guaranteed permanent territories of their own.

Third, an inspection board should be created to insure that funds, goods, and services promised to the Indians should be delivered to them. All too often, as had been the case with the Minnesota Dakotas, corruption and inefficiency resulted in the delay or even the theft of money and goods.

Fourth, a permanent Indian commission composed of whites and educated Indians should be created. The job of the commission would be to convince the Indians that they needed to maintain permanent peace with the whites and "adopt the habits and modes of civilized communities."

Although his plan received high praise, a bill containing his four points never reached Congress. But Ely Parker, who had a deeper grasp than most of Indian Affairs, was being heard more and more, not just in Grant's circle of advisers but around the nation.

His place in Grant's staff—to Ely's great sorrow—became even more important in March 1866. His friend Colonel Theodore "Joe" Bowers, who was Grant's adjutant, died in a freak accident. While on a visit to West Point, he tripped and was run over by a railroad car. After he and Grant attended their friend Joe's funeral, Ely took Bowers's place as Grant's aide-de-camp.

Although Ely was still returning to New York now and then, his real home was with the army and Grant. He turned his farm in Tonawanda over to his brother Nic. Meanwhile, Grant, who became general-in-chief of the army that July, raised his Indian aide in rank, first as a second lieutenant in the regular army and then, by stages, to captain, major, colonel, and brigadier general.

The Indian who had longed for his native woods as a teenage visitor was now quite at home in Washington. He drove about the capital with a fine team of black horses and attended functions at the White House as an honored guest. Although he was sent on an extended mission to the west in April 1867 to prevent the conflict with the "hostile Sioux" from spreading, he involved himself again in Washington's social life on his return to the capital in November.

In fact, he was more involved than most suspected. In December 1867, Washington society was suddenly abuzz with unexpected news. The Indian general was engaged to be married. That in itself was a surprise. Now thirty-nine, Ely had been seen by most as a confirmed bachelor. But what was even more of a shock was the identity of his intended bride. She was Minnie Orton Sackett, one of

MINNIE ORTON SACKETT

the city's most eligible belles. She was white, strikingly lovely, and only eighteen years old.

Although the story of how they first met was never made public, it may have been through Ely's acquaintance with her mother. Anna Sackett's husband was a lieutenant colonel in the 9th New York Cavalry who was wounded and taken prisoner on June 11, 1864. Mrs. Sackett, herself a well-off Washingtonian, had arrived at City Point a month later, delivering a wagon full of meats, canned fruits, and other supplies for the men of the 9th New York Cavalry. She approached Grant, asking him to write to General Lee asking for permission to visit her husband behind enemy lines. Lee replied that he would inquire about her husband, who, it turned out, had died of his wounds a few days after his capture.

At that point in the war, Ely Parker was always at Grant's side, and it's likely the letter to Lee was written by him. Perhaps Ely's quiet competence then impressed Mrs. Sackett. Perhaps, too, after the war she was the one who introduced her daughter Minnie to the courtly Indian officer at one of the social functions they attended.

People described Minnie as a happy and lively young woman, modest and accomplished. There were other suitors. And when the man she chose was not of her race, they were deeply disappointed— to the point where it's said threats were made against Ely's life.

The wedding was planned for December 17 at the Episcopal Church of the Epiphany in Washington. Built in 1844 in the Gothic style, it was a spectacular place for a wedding that was bound to be well attended, especially since none other than General Grant was to give the bride away.

General Grant, his staff, and virtually all of Washington society was there that Sunday for the grand event. But the groom was not. The last time Ely had been seen was the day before when he borrowed a military sash from General Grant. Wild rumors spread about what had happened to him, ranging from murder and suicide to wild rumors about Ely's absconding because he was already married to another woman back in western New York.

Two days later, the missing groom appeared. Ely was alive and well, but had what some felt was a fantastic tale to tell. After borrowing that sash, he said, he'd been met by another New York Indian. Invited to have a celebratory glass of wine at the other man's room, Ely had been drugged and only awoke the day after the wedding.

Ely said the man, whose identity he never disclosed, was a follower of the Handsome Lake religion, which forbade racial intermarriage.

Others explained Ely's failure to appear on quite another cause. They believed he had gone out on a four-day drunk and in his inebriated state forgot all about the wedding. Yet again, that stereotype of the drunken Indian reared its ugly head to damage Ely's reputation.

It was clear that Ely had fences to mend—not only with his bride-to-be and her mother, but with his friend and commanding officer. Apparently, whatever Ely said was convincing enough that he was forgiven. The wedding was rescheduled for December 24. An even larger crowd came for the event than the last time, most of them curiosity seekers and the press. It was estimated by the Washington newspapers that three thousand people gathered at the church that day.

This time, not only the groom was missing, but so, too, was the bride. Ely and Minnie had been quietly wed the evening before. Only a few were there, including Grant, who gave the bride away. The new Mr. and Mrs. Parker had left that night to honeymoon in New York City and Rochester.

The reason for that early ceremony, according to Ely's grand-nephew Arthur C. Parker, was that a plot had been hatched to

assassinate the bridegroom before he would reach the altar. Whether or not that was true, Ely was finally married. Happily so, in a union that would last for twenty-eight years—the rest of his life.

When asked after her husband's passing about her reason for marrying an Indian, Minnie's answer was a straightforward one.

"Some people thought I married the General because he was an Indian . . . I married the General because I loved him."

THE INDIAN COMMISSIONER

The Indian is the ward of the Government. The management and direction of all his affairs and relations in a civil capacity has been conferred by the act of 1832 exclusively upon this Office . . .

—ELY PARKER TO JACOB COX,
SECRETARY OF THE INTERIOR

N ot long after Ely's marriage, another event occurred that elevated his rainbow even higher in the circles of American government. His friend General Grant was elected president of the United States. As in the past, Grant was loyal to his friends and brought many of them with him into the government— regardless of their competency. As a result, his would be regarded as one of the most corrupt administrations in U.S. history.

Among those Grant wished to bring with him, of course, was his close companion Ely Parker. Ely was to be the new commissioner of Indian Affairs. Unlike some of Grant's appointees, there was no doubt about Ely's qualifications or ability to handle this difficult assignment. His excellent service for the past two years in dealing with the western tribes had proven his competence.

Senator John Thayer of Nebraska was among those who approved of Grant's choice. Regarded as an expert on Indian affairs—as a former Indian fighter in the army—Thayer stated that he could "think of no one whose appointment to this position would give greater satisfaction to the country."

But there were two major hurdles that Ely still had to clear— and both of them had to do entirely with his being an Indian.

The first was that same old stereotype of all Indians being unreliable because of their supposed addiction to alcohol. There were rumors around Washington, which may have been baseless, that Ely Parker had "habits, in the manner of drinking." However, when Asher Wright, a missionary who'd spent his life among the Tonawandas, was asked his opinion of Ely Parker, his response was positive.

Wright said he believed that Ely Parker's "appointment will break up the system of plunder which has been a disgrace to the country and ruinous to the Indian." In fact, Wright added, "Grant could not do better than to appoint him."

The second hurdle that Ely had to clear was one that he had tried unsuccessfully to clear when it confronted him earlier in life. As an Indian, he was not a citizen and thus not eligible to hold such an office. It was true that a civil rights act had been passed in 1866 after the war. It granted citizenship to all persons born in the United States, regardless of race, color, or other previous conditions or servitude. Native Americans, though, who were legally exempted by the Constitution—which referred to them as "Indians not taxed"—were excluded.

This time, it was not a barrier that kept Ely Parker out. With Grant, the president of the United States, on his side, a way was found to interpret that law. It was pointed out that General Ely S. Parker was not living on a reservation. He was living as a citizen. Grant's new attorney general, Ebenezer Hoar, then ruled that Ely was qualified to serve as Indian commissioner.

Nominated by Grant on April 13, 1869, the Senate confirmed it the next day on a vote of 36–12. Ely was now the first Native American to hold an office in American government.

Few jobs in Grant's government were more crucial and complicated than his. His organization's policies did not just impact the lives of the 300,000 Native Americans in the United States and its territories. They affected the peace and settlement of the American West. Non-Indian and Indian lives were both at stake. During the Dakota War, four hundred or more white civilian settlers had been killed. Preventing anything like that—or the terrible Sand Creek massacre—could rest on Ely's decisions.

One of Ely's main problems was the so-called "Indian Ring," corrupt officials conspiring with military contractors to cheat the government and make huge sums for themselves. Since the focus of the military after 1865 was on the West and potentially hostile Indians, that was where the money was to be made. A contractor might agree to provide cattle for food—as required by treaty—to a particular group of Indians. He would drive the herd to a reservation, where the dishonest Indian agent would accept delivery so that the contractor could be paid. After receiving payment, the contractor would pay the agent a bribe and then take that same herd and drive it to another reservation to repeat the process again. And in the meantime, the Indians would remain unfed.

There's a quote from an unnamed Indian chief of the time that exemplifies how it was. Supposedly, the old man said this to General William Sherman about his former Indian agent: "When he came he brought everything in a little bag, when he left it took two steamboats to carry away his things."

The Office of Indian Affairs that Ely now headed was a large agency. He had no fewer than thirty-eight clerks, seventy Indian agents responsible for interacting with individual tribes, and fifteen superintendents to whom those agents reported. There were farmers, doctors, skilled and unskilled workers of all kinds. In all, more than six hundred people were employed in the nation's capital and in the field.

One of the first actions taken by Ely was an attempt to purge the Indian service of corrupt agents. Of all the religious groups that dealt with Native Americans, the Quakers—with their commitment to peace and universal brotherhood—had the best record and were often regarded by Native tribes as trustworthy. Some of the ideas put forward in the Good Message by Handsome Lake may have come from his contact with a Quaker missionary. Before Grant was inaugurated, groups of Quakers had approached him about serving as agents. Ely embraced that idea and began what became called the Quaker Policy. Before long, fourteen of the seventy Indian agents were Quakers and two of the fifteen superintendent jobs were staffed by Quakers. Groups of Quakers were given a hand in not only nominating agents and superintendents, but also in overseeing their work.

Aside from the Quakers, who were trusted by both Grant and Ely for their honesty and peacefulness, neither the president nor his new Indian commissioner trusted civilians as much as they did the military. Transferring the Indian office back from the Interior to the War Department (where their trusted friend John Rawlins—though ailing—was now secretary of war) was not possible politically. However, appointing army officers as Indian agents and superintendents was something that they could do. Before long, nearly all of the old politically appointed agents and superintendents had been replaced by army officers and Quakers.

Parker's instructions to his new appointees were quite direct. They were to help the Indians prepare for "the inevitable change of their mode of life . . . keep constantly before their minds the pacific intentions of the government, and obtain their confidence by acts of kindness and honesty and justly dealing with them . . ."

Ely had suggested in 1867, two years before taking his post, that a board of inspection should be created. Its job would be to oversee the Indian agencies and root out corrupt practices. In 1869, as president, Grant did just that. A Board of Indian Commissioners was established. The ten men of that board, "eminent for their intelligence and philanthropy," were empowered to inspect the Indian agencies and advise the government on its Indian policies. With

Ely's encouragement, they immediately began visiting the Native American reservations around the country to view conditions and point out abuses.

While intelligent and philanthropic, those ten men also had another agenda. All of them were white Protestants and forceful in their belief in the superiority of Christianity. That was reflected in their first annual report, which stated bluntly that "the religion of our blessed Saviour is believed to be the most effective agent for the civilization of any people." It appears that no one on the board was more self-righteous or certain of his position than the Philadelphia merchant and militant Episcopalian who was elected its chairman. His name—which Ely would get to know far too well—was William Welsh.

WILLIAM WELSH

Providing the Indians with supplies was one of Ely's main concerns as commissioner. Now that they were confined to reservations, unable to rely on such traditional ways of subsistence as hunting, the tribes would not remain peaceful unless supplied with food, clothing, agricultural implements, and other supplies. This was where much of the fraud had taken place in the past. Exorbitant prices were paid for goods that were often not actually supplied or were stolen before reaching the reservations. Ely went personally to New York and Philadelphia to oversee those purchases and employed trusted inspectors to help him ensure honesty.

On his first trip to New York City, however, Ely ran into a problem that would dog him throughout his tenure as Indian commissioner. Because he was an Indian himself, some members of the Board of Inspectors did not trust him. One of those board members, George Hayes Stuart, a Philadelphia banker, showed up. Ely and his inspectors had already certified and packed the supplies for shipment west, but Stuart would not accept that. He demanded that everything be moved to another warehouse where he would have everything unpacked and inspected by Stuart himself.

Ely was alarmed. The supplies were desperately needed. Moving, unpacking, and reinspecting hundreds of crates could take weeks. He rushed to Washington. There he was assured by Cox, the secretary of the interior, and Grant himself that Ely and his own team of inspectors were the only ones who could certify the supplies and authorize paying the merchant.

The members of the Board of Indian Commissioners were

outraged. William Welsh, the chairman, stated that "more than suspected fraud" was likely and inferred that "the Indian" was part of it. But Grant was adamant. His commissioner, Ely S. Parker, was the final authority in the expenditure of all appropriations for the Indians approved by Congress. Welsh resigned from the board to "work for the Indians in his own way." Ely had won his first victory in his new job. However, it came at the cost of making an enemy.

The next two years were ones of both joy and sorrow for Ely.

The immediate sorrow that came soon after his appointment was the passing of his dear friend Rawlins. From the description of his symptoms—losing weight and strength, a persistent cough often producing blood—it seems he was suffering from tuberculosis. It was, in the mid-nineteenth century, a disease for which there was no cure. Six months into his term as secretary of war, John Rawlins lay dying. Ely was by his side and he found himself once again serving as a secretary to a military friend as Rawlins dictated his will to him. One of the saddest parts of Rawlins's passing was that Grant never showed up to bid him farewell. "Hasn't the old man come yet?" Rawlins kept asking. Years later, in a confidential letter to John E. Smith, Ely would blame Grant's West Point comrades, who told Grant to distance himself from his old friend. They, and Grant's status-conscious wife, saw Rawlins, despite his service to Grant, as beneath them.

But the joy coming Ely's way was visible to everyone. After all his years of bachelorhood, he was once again displaying his ability to adapt to any challenge. By all accounts he was fully enjoying his new role as the husband of a Washington socialite. His marriage to Minnie was bringing him even more into the center of Washington's social life, including frequent visits to Grant's White House. "General Parker and his little, decidedly pronounced blonde wife" were welcomed at all sorts of events. Poised and elegant, clearly devoted to her husband, Minnie Parker was—as one newspaper reporter put it—"said to entertain as well as any lady in Washington."

Not everyone, however, welcomed the sight of a dark-skinned Indian by the side of a white woman. One columnist, herself a woman, wrote in a story published in February 1870 in the *New York Herald*:

> His wife is fair, standing beside him and attracts attention because she has broken a law; but why should she be received in society for the same reason that puts the poor Irish washerwoman who links her fate with another race, beyond the pale of association, only the newspapers can answer. And yet no half breeds have made their appearance, which proves there is a destiny which has something to do with shaping our ends.

Ely seems to have ignored, or at least not reacted to such overt racism. He also appears to have paid little attention to the things being said about him by William Welsh. Welsh was making visits on his own to the western tribes in support of the work being done by the Episcopal Church. That Christianizing work pleased him. "Our holy religion will soon displace the superstitious rites that are fast losing their influence over the heathen people." But Welsh also conducted his own investigations into the provision of supplies and came back to Washington convinced that fraud was still taking place and that Ely was party to it.

Welsh confided his suspicions at length to Edward P. Smith, a Congregational minister recently appointed to head an Indian Agency. Smith, who would in 1873 be appointed by Grant as commissioner of Indian Affairs, was not impressed. He found Welsh to be insufferably grandiose—giving Smith "a full report of his past life to date." Welsh had no proof of any wrongdoing because the speculators were "covering their tracks." However, he was certain that "Colonel Parker is very closely in with the ring." Smith left their meeting convinced of two things. The first was that not constantly consulting with William Welsh was Commissioner Parker's only sin. The second was that it was quite possible that Colonel Parker would soon have to leave his position.

Despite Grant's peace policy and Ely's frequent visits to the western reservations, relations with the western tribes remained troubled. At the end of 1869 Ely reported that hostilities, though not overt war, still existed. And near the start of the new year the army responded to complaints about thefts and a murder on the part of the Piegans in Montana. That response was brutal and out of proportion to any crimes that might have been committed. In a morning raid on a sleeping camp along the Marias River, Major Eugene M. Baker and his troops—in what became known as the Marias Massacre, or the Baker Massacre—killed between 173 and 217 Piegans. Most of them were women, children, and elders. Further, the Piegan camp attacked was a peaceful one. Led by Chief Heavy Runner, they had been promised protection by the United States government. Their only crime was that they were said to be harboring a man who'd killed a white rancher.

Ely's public response to the military action was unsympathetic to the Piegans. "Although the consequences were deplorable, yet they were effectual in completely subduing the Indians, and the entire nation has since not only been quiet, but even solicitous to enter into arrangements for permanent peace and good behavior in the future."

However, there was even more of a shift toward desiring peace in the Grant administration's Indian policies following the tragic event. And Ely himself became even more proactive at doing whatever he could to prevent hostilities. So much so, in fact, that his job and reputation would soon be at stake.

That summer of 1870 saw the possibility of more trouble. Red Cloud, one of the most important leaders of the Oglala Lakotas, had led a successful campaign against the United States military from 1866 to 1868. It had resulted in the abandonment of several forts and the withdrawal of American troops from Red Cloud's territory. Although he had signed the Treaty of Fort Laramie in 1868, trouble seemed to again be brewing. Parker's agent at Crow Creek had asked for military protection. A major war against the most powerful of all the Indian nations seemed possible.

Ely suggested—instead of military action—bringing some of the Lakota chiefs to Washington to hear their grievances. Grant agreed. On June 1, Red Cloud and sixteen other Lakota leaders arrived in the capital. In the negotiations that followed, Red Cloud expressed his dissatisfaction with the reservation and complained that his people were now "poor and naked." Those concerns would be eloquently presented by him a few days later in a now-famous speech at Cooper Union in New York City.

CHIEF RED CLOUD SPEAKING AT COOPER UNION, NEW YORK CITY, 1870

During their consultation with the Lakota leaders in Washington, Jacob Dolson Cox, the secretary of the interior, held up Ely Parker as an example.

Here is the Commissioner of Indian Affairs, who is a chief among us. He belonged to a race who lived here long

before the white man came to this country. He now has power and white people obey him and he directs what shall be done in very important business. We will be brethren to you in the same way if you follow his good example and learn our civilization.

The negotiations with the Oglalas proved to be a success. Red Cloud returned home advocating peace. He and many of his band took no part in the war of 1876 to 1877 led by such men as Crazy Horse and Sitting Bull. The remainder of that year of 1870 saw no further troubles with the western tribes. It was due in large part to the timely delivery of promised supplies to Native American communities now relying—as promised by treaties—on the American government to avoid starvation. Although Congress had not adopted Ely's four-point peace plan, Grant had and it was working.

Another of Ely's ideas—the end of making treaties with Indians—was also instituted near the conclusion of his tenure in office. Ely had long held that the treaty system always resulted badly for the Indian. Treaties always favored the government. They were, as Ely expressed it, "like the handle to a jug. The advantages and power of execution are all on one side."

Most of all, Ely took pride in the fact that the country had been spared the expense of further Indian wars. (It's been estimated that the three expeditions in the Sioux Wars between 1866 and 1868 had cost $10 million. That might not seem like much until one considers that $1 in 1868 equals $175 today.) And there was, for the first time in centuries, something like peace between whites and Indians. That relative peace being enjoyed in 1870, Ely believed, was due in large part to his influence.

But in January 1871, the Indian who, as Cox put it, "now has power and white people obey him," found his own peace shattered. William Welsh wrote a letter to Columbus Delano, the new secretary of the interior, alleging that the Indian commissioner had defrauded the government in the purchase of supplies. The Appropriations Committee of the House of Representatives invited Welsh to press charges, which he readily did. Ely found himself on trial.

What had led to those charges, aside from Welsh's hatred of Ely? It was one particular action on Ely's part. After Red Cloud's return home, there were severe shortages of supplies along the Missouri River. Food needed to be purchased and shipped immediately or the Indians would leave the reservations and hostilities would begin. As Ely said, "It was only the food and clothing that kept them about the agencies." The situation was so desperate that the governor of the Dakota Territory stated bluntly that there were only two choices: "We must feed or fight the Indians."

However, an appropriations bill had not been passed by Congress—and would not eventually be passed until weeks later. Ely made emergency arrangements with a trusted contractor, James Bosler, to provide food, flour, and other supplies with the promise that he would be paid when the funds were appropriated. The food was delivered and the crisis averted.

What Ely had done was both admirable and understandable. There's little doubt that a war was averted and lives were saved. But he had circumvented Congress and not consulted the Board of Indian Commissioners before arranging the provision of supplies.

Ely defended himself clearly and confidently. The law requiring him to consult with the board was not passed until after he

took that action. The money to purchase the supplies had eventually been approved and the payment made after that approval. Still, the charges shook him deeply and he became ill with what may have been a recurrence of the malaria contracted during the war.

NORTON P. CHIPMAN

When the investigation

began, Ely chose to be represented by counsel. The person he chose was Norton P. Chipman. It was a wise choice. Chipman had served as judge advocate in the army. It was Chipman who had served as lead prosecutor in the trial of Henry Wirz. Wirz, who ended up being executed for his crimes, had been the commander of Andersonville, the horrific southern prison camp. He was one of only two people tried for war crimes during the Civil War.

There was another reason why Ely put his faith in Chipman. He was a fellow Mason.

In the trial that followed, Welsh was allowed to testify and question witnesses. As before, Welsh testified that he had no proof because the offenders had covered their tracks so well. He implied that Ely was a drunk and unfit for office as one but a generation removed from barbarism. Chipman was straightforward in Ely's defense. He pointed out that Ely had acted in an emergency in his purchase of supplies. In similar circumstances General Sherman and General William Harney had done the same to placate the Indians, spending even more money than Ely did. Chipman produced documents proving Ely's actions had been known by Cox, the secretary of the interior, who had raised no objection.

When the committee published its report, it agreed there had been an emergency. Ely was criticized for not consulting the president before making the arrangements to purchase the supplies. There were faults in the Indian office, "irregularities, neglect, and incompetence," but no dishonesty. The conclusion of the report was very clear about that. It stated, "We have no evidence of any pecuniary or financial advantage sought or derived by the Commissioner, or any one connected with his Bureau."

Ely's honesty had been vindicated, but a new law was passed following his trial. It gave broad powers to the Board of Indian Commissioners, requiring that every purchase be approved first by the board. In essence, Ely was stripped of much of his power and would have to do whatever the board told him to do.

On August 1, 1871, Ely submitted his resignation to President Grant.

Seeing that Parker's position was untenable because of the Indian Board's continual hostility toward the Indian in office, Grant regretfully accepted Ely's stepping down.

"Your resignation," Grant wrote, "severs official relations which have existed between us for eight consecutive years without cause of complaint as to your entire fitness for either of the important places which you have had during that time."

Once again, as had happened too many times before, Ely found his rainbow broken at its height. Where would he go now?

I AM
A MAN

Why should you test the capacity of the red man's mind
in measure that may have an improper scale? Do you
measure cloth with a balance or by the gallon?

—ELY PARKER TO
JAMES E. KELLY, SCULPTOR

E ly Parker was now forty-three years old. His career in government service was over. At a time in life when most men had either established themselves or accepted their lot, he had to start again. (The average life expectancy of a man in 1871 in the United States was only thirty-nine.)

Few men, though, had Ely's incredible ability to adapt in adversity. Nor did they have the sort of contacts he had. Not only could he turn to the officers he had served with in the war, he could also rely on the friends from Yates Academy with whom he had maintained close ties through constant correspondence. Plus, as always, he had his brother Masons, who viewed him with the greatest respect.

Another thing in Ely's favor was the social circle he had become connected to through his marriage to Minnie. That proved to be an immediate advantage. Minnie's loyal friends included Josephine Jones Brown, described as "one of the reigning belles of Washington." Her marriage to Arthur Brown, a Wall Street investor, had resulted

ROBIN'S NEST, FAIRFIELD, CONNECTICUT

in her moving to Connecticut, where her husband had a mansion. (Brown's wealth had come in part from his father, a famous shipbuilder. The America's Cup races are named after his yacht *America*.)

At what was likely a suggestion from the Browns, Ely and Minnie moved to Connecticut. They purchased a large, beautiful home on the main street in Fairfield. Robin's Nest is what they called it. For the next five years Robin's Nest was their primary residence while Ely followed his new career as an investor. Like many other well-to-do businessmen, he seems to have pursued a number of different investments. The first was acquiring an interest in the Read Carpet Company of Bridgeport, Connecticut, in partnership with their friend Brown. Other investment opportunities followed. Ely's Yates schoolmate Henry M. Flagler was now a director and original shareholder in a new business called Standard Oil. The house next door to Robin's Nest was owned by Oliver Burr Jennings. Jennings was another of Standard Oil's directors and shareholders and married to the sister of William Rockefeller. William, with his more famous brother John D. Rockefeller, was one of the founders of Standard Oil.

With such connections as these, Ely began to amass a considerable fortune. Each morning, alongside other wealthy briefcase-carrying commuters in suits, he would board the New York and New Haven Railroad for New York City to return that evening after a

day's work in the metropolis. He and Minnie were also maintaining a second residence in the city and they would sometimes refer to the Fairfield mansion as their "summer place."

This way of life seemed to suit Ely well. Another of his neighbors, George Mills, described him as "a widely read man" who was "modest and retiring and despite his glamorous life, had little to say about himself, unless drawn out." Mills further recollected that Ely's "span of horses paced through the little Fairfield streets like a circus rider in the Colosseum. His footman and coachman were distinctly, but tastefully caparisoned, and when he sometimes attended band concerts in Seaside Park in the fashion of the era, all eyes were turned toward the distinguished Indian."

Ely seems to have done little in those Fairfield years to stay in touch with anyone in the Tonawanda community other than his brother Nic. Nic was still running the family farm on the land that had been given to Ely by the Tonawandas. Ely's only request had been that whenever Nic had black horses that seemed likely and spirited enough to suit his brother, he would have them sent to Connecticut. For a time, Ely and Minnie hosted Nic's teenage daughter, who had been named Minnie after her young aunt, who adored her.

ELY, CIRCA 1870

But young Minnie was not at ease in "this white man's heaven" and returned to the reservation after a short stay.

All seemed perfect for Ely in his new life. But then, in 1873, a reversal of his fortunes began. After agreeing to be bondsman for a bank cashier, the man embezzled a large sum of money and then vanished. Ely was called upon to repay those funds.

Arthur C. Parker described what happened next:

> General Parker's lawyers hastened to him with advice. "You won't have to pay," they said. "You are an Indian, and the law does not hold you to it. You can not be held by law to live up to that bond. It is not worth the paper it was written on." Here was a loop-hole that would save the accumulation of a lifetime. The elements of escape were few and simple: "Indian, do not have to pay, law can not compel—contract void."
>
> But General Parker gave a single answer, "I fully intend to make that bond good. I executed it in good faith. I am a man and if the law does not compel me to pay, my honor does." And he paid, though his fortune was wrecked.

Although his financial loss was great, to say that Ely's fortune was wrecked was an exaggeration. He and Minnie kept their home in Fairfield for more than ten years after that. However, this was not his only financial misfortune in the volatile markets of the time. One of the saddest losses, not just for Ely, but for the nation, was the collapse of the Freedman's Bank. Established in 1865 to assist former slaves in their transition to freedom, the Freedman's Savings and Trust had thirty-seven branches throughout eleven states, mostly run on the ground level by African Americans. However, in 1874, it was discovered that fraud on the part of white men in the upper management had destabilized the institution. Millions of dollars were lost to the African Americans who had entrusted their savings and to those, like Ely, who had invested in it.

Just the year before, in the Panic of 1873, Ely had also lost money in the failure of the bank Jay Cooke and Company—which had helped the North bankroll the Civil War. While still relatively well off, Ely was no longer wealthy and needed to find further employment.

Ely tried to turn back to his old profession of engineering, but found that few jobs were available for him. It was now fifteen years since he'd been a government engineer in Dubuque. "While I was soldiering," he wrote, "the profession ran away from me, other and younger men had stepped in and filled the places."

Once again, a friend from the past helped him find a job. In this case it was someone who knew Ely both from his work as a government engineer and during the Civil War—William F. Smith. In 1857, during Ely's brief posting in Detroit before going to Galena, William F. Smith was the army engineer who'd supervised his work for the Light House Board and it was to Smith that Ely had first been assigned as an adjutant in the war. Retired from the army, the former brigadier general was now serving on the Board of Commissioners of the New York City Police Department as its president. With Smith's recommendation, on September 30, 1876, Ely S. Parker, former head engineer, Grand Sachem of the Iroquois, and retired brevet general, was appointed as a clerk for the New York City Police Department.

His salary was modest, $2,400 a year—equal to about $45,000 in twenty-first-century dollars. However, it was quite likely assisted by savings and what investments he and Minnie still had. Even though Ely's salary was later cut to a meager $2,000 a year as part of an economy measure affecting the whole police department, their income was sufficient for them to keep their "summer home" in Fairfield and a residence on West Forty-Second Street in New York City and to visit expensive resorts during vacations.

Ely's clerical position—which he held for nineteen years, the rest of his life—kept him very busy. He worked for the Committee on Repairs and Supplies, drawing up contracts and keeping meticulous records. While his position was less than intellectually challenging, he was a celebrity to many of his fellow workers and was often visited by writers at his home, eager to hear of his experiences. The one person he was no longer seeing was his former patron and collaborator, Lewis Henry Morgan. The two had drifted apart after the war. Morgan had applied for the post that Ely gained as Indian commissioner, and after that, the two never spoke while Ely was in Washington. Morgan, though, maintained a warm relationship with Ely's Tonawanda relatives. While still involved in ethnological pursuits, Morgan was also focused on his own political career as a New York State senator and being a wealthy investor.

Ely joined and took regular part in such organizations of Civil War veterans as the Grand Army of the Republic and the Military Order of the Loyal Legion of the United States. He was still invited to speak at Masonic gatherings—displaying and telling the story of the Red Jacket medal as he always did. But he was becoming much more dedicated to his place among other veterans. Now that he was no longer Indian commissioner, he had little to do with national Indian affairs.

Though Ely's home was far from Tonawanda, he was not totally inactive as a Seneca sachem. Apparently he was regarded as valuable enough by the Tonawandas for the clan mothers to not "take away his horns." He did, on occasion, go to Washington to represent Seneca interests—as in 1878, when he went to the Indian Office to gain permission for the Allegheny Reservation to lease some oil wells. And he made occasional visits to Tonawanda, where he could, by speaking Seneca, "loosen up my tongue." But his most regular contact with other Indians was with his siblings. Ely's lot had changed. His life was now largely thrown in with the white man's world.

MAUDE PARKER, DATES UNKNOWN

His life also changed in another way—one that delighted him. Two years after beginning his new career as a civilian employee with the New York City Police Department, on August 14, 1878, Minnie gave birth to their daughter, Maud Theresa Parker. Ely and Minnie both adored her. Although she was one of those "half-breeds" of whom certain Washington writers had spoken so cynically, she was not regarded as Haudenosaunee by anyone at Tonawanda. Indian identity among the Iroquois always comes solely through the mother's line. Still, some of her father's stubborn pride seems to have been inherited by Maud. Ely called her Ahweh-ee-yo, which means "Beautiful Flower." When, as a little girl, she was teased about her ancestry by playmates, her response was "I'm a real American and the only one here."

Over the years, more and more people came to Ely to ask him about his war experiences, but he was reticent to discuss them. Too many articles and books were being written now about the war—and Grant's part in it. Ely was disgusted by, as he put it, "the perfect diarrhea of war papers and the innumerable controversies" they stirred up. The one topic he did address, now and then, was the character of his friend and former commander, whose reputation was being vilified by some (southern sympathizers, in particular) who described him as inept and a hopeless drunk. Ely knew what it was to be accused in that way. In 1889 he spoke before the Loyal Legion on "The

Character of Grant," defending the general to whom he'd been so close.

His meetings with Grant, after leaving Washington, were infrequent and short, but pleasant. In 1880, he visited Grant at his home in New York City, taking with him his copy of the draft of the famous surrender at Appomattox. Grant certified it as authentic, writing on it that the document was one of the original impressions from the manifold. Upon Grant's death in 1885, Ely was part of the funeral procession and wrote a note to Grant's son Fred saying, "I loved your father deeply, deeply and sincerely."

However, despite that statement, Ely and the other men of his staff who'd been close to Grant in the war and during the early years in Washington after it ended felt they'd been pushed aside. Rawlins, Bowers, and Ely in particular felt wounded by Grant's neglect. In that confidential letter of 1886 to John E. Smith, Ely wrote that:

> There are a great many things that I could say of Grant and his friends, but which are better kept locked within my own bosom. I may say that the one great fault of his life was his abandonment of his early best and truest friends, and the taking unto him of false and strange gods who at last ruined him utterly . . . Politics was not his forte and his love of filthy lucre [money] floored him, Requiescat in pace.

ELY, CIRCA 1890

Although neglected by Grant on the one hand and unwilling to say much about his war years on the other, Ely found himself in demand for quite another reason . . . his deep knowledge of his Seneca heritage and his unique ability to communicate that knowledge in English. Although he was far from the only person holding on to such information, he—and to a lesser extent his brother Nic and sister, Carrie—was seen as the source of knowledge about the Indians of New York.

There are several reasons why Ely held that position, whether he wanted it or not. One, of course, was his visibility since his teenage years as a source of information, a "cultural informant," as ethnologists put it. His work with Morgan—which had also opened much wider the doors to the white man's world for the young Ely—had made his name known while still a teenager. (Morgan himself, by the time of his death in 1881, had become widely recognized and honored as a founder of the field of ethnology and an intellectual mentor to those who followed.)

A second reason, already alluded to in the previous paragraph, was that by his late teens Ely was speaking and writing English better than most native speakers of that European tongue. Others, still living on the reservations, might know more about Iroquois ways, but lacked the ability to express it in the words of the majority culture now surrounding them. A third reason is that, all through his life, unlike some culture bearers who believed part of their job was to be protective of their people's ways, Ely displayed an eager willingness to share what he knew.

There is a fourth reason, as well, why Ely was the Indian turned to. The pressure on Native Americans to give up their "heathen" ways was increasing. In 1879, the United States Indian Industrial School in Carlisle, Pennsylvania, was opened. It was the flagship for a new approach to solving the "Indian problem." Its mission—and that of the hundreds of Indian schools all around the country that followed—was nothing less than cultural genocide. Carlisle's founder, Richard Henry Pratt, expressed Carlisle's aim quite bluntly. Kill the Indian: Save the Man. Ely, firmly established and respected in the white man's world, could freely speak about his people's "vanishing" ways, while any Indian child in Carlisle who uttered a single word in a Native language might be not only reprimanded but beaten.

In 1900, five years after Ely's passing, a Carlisle-like Indian school was established on the Cattaraugus Reservation. That institution—the Thomas Asylum of Orphan and Destitute Indian Children—would prove to be even more brutal than Carlisle. Most of the Iroquois children there were neither orphans nor, by Iroquois standards, destitute. They had parents and grandparents who loved them and mourned when they were snatched away. Families at Tonawanda recalled the wagon from the Thomas Indian school visiting the reservation to collect children—who were sometimes hidden by parents and grandparents to keep them from being taken.

HARRIET MAXWELL CONVERSE

One of the most significant white people who had a passionate interest in New York Indians was Harriet Maxwell Converse. Born in 1836, she and her husband, Franklin, both originally came from Elmira, New York. Harriet's father and grandfather had been traders with the Indians and had been "adopted," as many friends of the Senecas were in those days. (There's a long tradition among many Native American nations of such strategic adoptions in which a European person who has either been a friend or might prove useful in the future is given one or another "Indian name" that is both complimentary and describes the role they might play.) Harriet's grandfather was given the name of Ta-se-wa-ya-ee, or Honest Trader.

The Parkers first met Harriet and her husband in 1881. The Converses lived on West Forty-Sixth Street in New York City, not far from Ely, Minnie, and Maud. The two families—with their shared interests in books and music—soon became close friends. Franklin was a talented and innovative musician who made it his life's work to popularize what had formerly been scorned as a "Negro instrument," the banjo. But what created a special bond between Harriet and Ely was her commitment to Indian rights. Few white people did more in the late nineteenth century to help protect the interests of the Iroquois than Harriet Maxwell Converse. Moreover, unlike many so-called "Friends of the Indian," she did not see their traditional ways as foolish and superstitious.

Harriet was a published poet and writer. With a great deal of input from Ely, she would write such historical volumes such as *The Religious Festivals of the Iroquois Indians* and *Myths and Legends of the New York Iroquois*. Although her style was florid and romanticized, there was no question about her sincerity. Much of her time and her personal wealth went into her efforts to aid New York State Indian causes.

Soon after the families met, even though they lived close by, Ely and Harriet began to write letters to each other—much like contemporary email exchanges. Harriet had been adopted into the Seneca Snipe Clan and so Ely addressed her as "the Snipe." She, in turn, called him "the Wolf" for his clan or, recognizing him as Grand Sachem, as Donehogawa.

Harriet's respect and her firm commitment to the actual welfare of his people began to waken something in Ely that may have been dormant. He talked freely in his letters about himself and his views on the treatment of Indians by the government. He stated that he no longer believed in the wholesale adoption of European ways, the breaking up of the reservations. The only thing now that would save the Indians of America was for them to hold on to their religious traditions and tribal organizations. "When they abandon their birth right for a mess of christian pottage they will then cease to be a distinctive people."

The 1880s was a crucial time for American Indians and Ely was seeing clearly the new threats being posed. An organization called (ironically) the Indian Rights Association was pushing for the reservations to be broken up and the land parceled out to individual Indians—with the "leftover" land then being opened to white settlers. Those who accepted allotted land, living separately from the tribe, would be granted citizenship. The resulting Dawes Act of 1887 was a disaster for Native Americans, especially in the Indian

Territory that became the state of Oklahoma. Millions of acres ended up being taken. One of those who helped push the Dawes Act was the same William Welsh who had brought about Ely's downfall as Indian commissioner.

A similar plan was put forward in 1891 in New York State called the Whipple Bill, designed to force the allocation of all remaining Iroquois lands in the state to individual heads of households and extinguish all Indian land claims. Harriet Maxwell Converse helped achieve the defeat of that bill. She also, in 1902, helped defeat a federal bill that would have forced the Seneca Nation to pay the then huge sum of $200,000 to the Ogden Land Company, which had still not given up its fight against the Tonawandas.

Harriet was also involved in a project dear to Ely's heart—the reinternment of the remains of Red Jacket. Red Jacket had originally been buried near his home, but there were persistent efforts on the part of white collectors to find his grave and dig him up. Keeping the skulls and bones of famous Indians was a grotesque obsession in the nineteenth and early twentieth centuries. Sometimes those skulls were sent to eminent scientists for study, sometimes they were just kept as a curiosity. Among the many Native Americans whose skulls ended up in the hands of collectors were the Seminole chief Osceola and the famous war Apache leader Geronimo. George

Copway, a well-known Ojibway writer and lecturer of the time, had exhumed Red Jacket's body—to give him a better burial—but his family had intervened and taken it. For a time, Red Jacket's bones were hidden in his step-daughter's home.

The Buffalo Historical Society now proposed Forest Lawn Cemetery as the great orator's last resting place. It was in Buffalo, on land once part of the stolen Buffalo Creek Reservation, and the Seneca Nation approved the plan. On October 8, 1884, Ely, accompanied by his sister, Carrie, and her husband and his brother Nic, came to pay last respects to their tribal ancestor. A mixed crowd including not only the Converses and other white people but also a number of Senecas, gathered for the ceremony. Ely, wearing full military dress, spoke in English while Nic, wearing traditional regalia, translated Ely's words into Seneca. Then, later that evening, Ely—wearing Red Jacket's medal—spoke again at the Buffalo Historical Society about the Seneca Nation and its history of allegiance to the United States.

A monument was proposed for Red Jacket's grave, and Ely sketched out a design for it—a broken tree meant to reflect the words spoken by the old man before his death. "I am an aged tree and can stand no longer . . ."

However, the donor who agreed to contribute $10,000 toward

the statue thought Ely's idea was too horrid and grotesque. Instead, a heroic statue of Red Jacket was placed atop the monument.

Ely and his family continued to spend their summers outside the city in their home in Fairfield until 1887, renting it to others for most of the rest of the year. But its upkeep eventually became too much for them and in 1887 the decision was made to sell it. Ely's library in Fairfield was admired by his neighbors and word went out that the Parkers would be auctioning off the contents of the house. Among Ely's books was a first edition of Henry Ward Beecher's sermons and a local minister hoped he might persuade Parker to part with it.

Ely delighted in telling the story of what happened next. "Some impish impulse," Ely wrote in a letter, impelled him to open a trunk, take out the traditional Seneca outfit he'd stored there, and put those clothes on. Then, still dressed in full regalia, he climbed the ladder to take down some of the books on a high shelf.

The door being open, the clergyman walked into the library. When he looked up and saw an Indian perched on a ladder above him, he turned pale, spun around, and scurried out the door.

In 1890, Ely was sixty-two and his health began to fail. A sore that refused to heal developed on his foot—a sign of diabetes, another disease without effective treatment in those days. He still worked at the police department and even made public appearances, but his condition was worsening. The loss of two of his siblings, Carrie in March of 1892 and Nic in May of that same year—both dying from strokes—saddened him. In that same year, he applied for a pension as a permanent invalid, but continued in his daily job at police headquarters.

In July 1893, while at work, Ely felt ill around noon and lay down on a couch, unable to move his left arm and leg. He asked for a doctor and ended up being taken to the New York Hospital. He had suffered the first of a series of strokes.

Although his speech and mind were not impaired, he was greatly weakened. Minnie, devoted as ever, did all she could, but could tell that the end was near.

"The General," she wrote to their friend, the poet William Cullen Bryant, "is improving slowly. His arm and leg are useless. I doubt if he is ever able to do for himself again." Yet, even in those sad circumstances, she still celebrated her husband, the love of her life, saying that "he rebels against his condition, proud to the last, and well he might be, for grander nobler man never lived."

The pension Ely was awarded was only $12 a month. Their savings was gone and they were desperate for money. Ely put up for auction most of his prized possessions, keeping only the Red

Jacket medal. In April 1895, the last of his siblings, Levi, passed on. Ely, Minnie, and Maud, now seventeen years old, went to stay with friends in Fairfield several times that summer. Ely had improved enough to walk, but his left side remained weak. He tried to go back to work. On August 27, he went to the police department, but he looked and felt so ill that the commissioners—who now included Grant's son Fred and a young man named Theodore Roosevelt— were concerned. They granted him a leave of absence and sent him home.

ELY WITH MAUD, 1895

Hoping that their beloved Connecticut might give him some solace, the Parkers went again to Fairfield, guests of their friends Arthur and Josephine Brown. There, on August 30, 1895, Ely Samuel Parker, Do-ne-ho-ga-wa, walked on.

The funeral took place at the home of the Browns. Ely's body, dressed in full military uniform, lay in a black casket. Ely's Indian family was represented by Levi's daughter and Nic's son. Fred Grant was there, along with other members of the New York City Police Department and representatives of the Loyal Legion, the Masons, and the Grand Army of the Republic. Harriet Maxwell Converse brought with her leading women and men of all the New York Iroquois nations except the Mohawks. After the full Episcopal service, his coffin was taken to Oak Lawn Cemetery nearby, where he was buried.

Ely had, more than anything else, worried about the fate of his beloved family after his death. Minnie and Maud were left with little more than a few pieces of furniture and the clothing on their backs. To raise enough to live on, Minnie sold the rest of Ely's library, his personal effects, and even the Red Jacket medal—which ended up at the Buffalo Historical Society, where it remains to this day.

But Ely's family was far from forgotten. The Loyal Legion paid

Minnie $2,000 for Ely's copy of Lee's terms of surrender. The United States Congress passed a special act giving her a monthly pension. Then, two years after Ely's passing, Minnie, now forty-eight, married James Tallmadge Van Rensselaer, a prominent New York attorney who was fifty-five years old. That marriage lasted only two years, when her new husband died, leaving Minnie a substantial inheritance.

Ely's body did not remain at Oak Lawn long. A plot in Forest Lawn Cemetery had been offered to Ely before his death by the Buffalo Historical Society. It was next to the graves of other well-known Senecas, most notably Red Jacket himself. The following year Minnie agreed to the reburial. On January 20, 1897, the body of Ely Parker found its final resting place below the statue of Red Jacket.

Ely had, as his mother's vision foretold, returned to the "ancient land of his ancestors," for the Forest Lawn Cemetery had been Seneca land, lost when the Buffalo Creek Reservation was taken from them.

During the reburial at Forest Lawn, Chauncey Abrams, a Seneca sachem, was among those who spoke. "We are much gratified," he said in Seneca, "to know that Do-ne-ho-ga-wa rests among his own people and not in a land of strangers."

ONE REAL AMERICAN

Although Ely Parker's earthly journey had ended, his name and his story would continue on among his own people and the white people alike.

The Tonawanda Seneca people, who fought so heroically—with so much help from the youthful Ha-sa-no-an-da—to keep their homeland, have continued on, well beyond the buying back of their own land from the rapacious Ogden Land Company.

They maintain their traditional form of government led by hereditary sachems selected by clan mothers and are a vital part of the still-surviving League of the Haudenosaunee. And, to this day, they remember Ely S. Parker, who carried the name of Do-ne-ho-ga-wa, a man who more than any other walked with honor in two worlds.

BURIAL OF ELY PARKER BELOW THE RED JACKET MONUMENT, 1897

TIMELINE

CIRCA 1758 · Birth of Red Jacket, famous Seneca orator and member of the Wolf Clan. His influence and the medal given to him by President George Washington would feature strongly in Ely Parker's life.

1786 · Birth of Ga-ont-gwut-twus, Elizabeth Johnson Parker, mother of Ely Parker.

CIRCA 1793 · Birth of Jo-ne-es-sto-wa, William Parker, father of Ely S. Parker.

CIRCA 1799 · Handsome Lake's visions, which lead to his creation of the Gai'wiio, or "Good Message."

1812–1814 · William Parker serves the United States in the War of 1812.

1828 · Birth of Ha-sa-no-an-da, Ely Samuel Parker.

JANUARY 20, 1830 · Death of Red Jacket.

CIRCA 1834 · Ely attends Baptist Mission School near the reservation.

1838 · Treaty providing for the sale of the four Seneca reservations to the Ogden Land Company.

CIRCA 1838–1840 · Ely is in Grand River in Ontario, Canada, to learn woodcraft.

1840 · Election of President Harrison.

1841 · Tyler becomes president when Harrison dies.

FALL 1842 · Ely admitted as a tuition-free student to Yates Academy, twenty miles north of Tonawanda. He also is now working as an interpreter for the Tonawanda chiefs and writing documents for them.

1842 · Compromise Treaty saving the Seneca reservations at Cattaraugus and Allegheny, but providing for the sale of the reservations at Buffalo Creek and Tonawanda. Senecas are supposed to be removed to western lands by April 1, 1846.

APRIL 1844 · Parker meets Lewis Henry Morgan in a bookstore in Albany, New York.

1844 · Election of President Polk.

OCTOBER 1845 · Lewis Henry Morgan visits the Tonawanda Reservation for the first time.

OCTOBER 1845 · Ely enters Cayuga Academy in Aurora, New York.

FEBRUARY 1846 · Ely's first of many trips to Washington, D.C., as interpreter for the Seneca delegation of chiefs in their efforts to save the Tonawanda Reservation.

1846–1848 · Mexican-American War.

1847 · Ely accepts a position to study law and assist William P. Angel, the subagent for the New York State Indians. He moves to Ellicottville, New York.

1847 · Ely accepted as a member of Batavia Lodge No. 88 of the Free and Accepted Masons.

MAY 1847 · A party of approximately 160 New York Indians leave for the western lands allotted to them. Within four months, eighty are dead.

SUMMER 1848 · William Angel is removed from his post as subagent because he is not a "good Democrat." Ely is blocked from becoming a lawyer because he is not a "natural-born" or naturalized citizen.

TIMELINE

1848 · Election of President Taylor.

1849 · With Morgan's help, Ely obtains a position with an engineering party working on the Genesee Valley Canal.

SPRING 1850 · Ely moves to Rochester to continue his engineering work on New York Canals. Eventually gains the position of engineer.

1851 · Publication of *League of the Ho-De-no-sau-nee, or Iroquois* by Lewis Henry Morgan.

SEPTEMBER 19, 1851 · Ely is selected by the Tonawanda Council to take the place of Chief John Blacksmith, who died. Ely becomes one of the fifty royaners, or sachems, of the Iroquois League, with the name of Donehogawa. Although only one of the Iroquois "chiefs," he is now referred to as (and calls himself) the "Grand Sachem of the Six Nations"—at the young age of twenty-three. He is also invested with the Red Jacket medal.

JANUARY 1853 · New York governor Horatio Seymour formally recognizes Ely as the "elected chief and Representative . . . of the Six Nations."

CIRCA 1853 · Ely begins to be involved with the New York State Militia; becomes a captain of engineers with the Rochester 54th Regiment.

JULY 23, 1855 · Ely accepts a position as chief engineer for the construction of a ship canal in the South; moves to Norfolk, Virginia.

MARCH 4, 1857 · Ely appointed by the U.S. Treasury Department as superintendent of lighthouse construction on the upper Great Lakes.

TIMELINE

MARCH 5, 1857 · Supreme Court rules that the federal government will take no action to remove the Tonawanda Senecas from their land.

APRIL 6, 1857 · Ely arrives in Galena, Illinois.

NOVEMBER 5, 1857 · United States–Tonawanda treaty allowing the Tonawanda Senecas to buy back about three-fifths of their land.

1860 · Ely meets and befriends Ulysses S. Grant, who was then working in his father's store in Galena.

1860 · Election of President Lincoln.

MARCH 26, 1861 · Ely removed from his position as superintendent of engineers and replaced by a political appointee. He returns to New York State to the Tonawanda Reservation.

APRIL 12, 1861 · American Civil War begins. Ely, now farming family land at Tonawanda, repeatedly attempts to enlist but is refused because he is an Indian.

FEBRUARY 23, 1862 · Death of Ely's mother.

MAY 25, 1863 · Ely is finally commissioned as an assistant adjutant general of engineers. He leaves Tonawanda and joins General John E. Smith's division near Vicksburg, Mississippi.

SEPTEMBER 18, 1863 · Ely is assigned to the personal military staff of General Grant.

1864 · Death of Ely's father.

APRIL 9, 1865: Ely is present at General Robert E. Lee's surrender and writes out the terms of surrender.

TIMELINE

APRIL 14, 1865 · President Lincoln is assassinated. Ely remains on his military staff, advising Grant and the War Department about Indian Affairs.

DECEMBER 23, 1867 · Ely marries Minnie Sackett.

MARCH 4, 1869 · Grant inaugurated as president.

APRIL 26, 1869 · Ely resigns from the military to become commissioner of Indian Affairs.

AUGUST 1, 1871 · Ely submits his resignation as commissioner of Indian Affairs.

SEPTEMBER 1871 · Ely and Minnie move to Fairfield, Connecticut. He becomes a successful Wall Street investor.

SEPTEMBER 30, 1876 · After losses in the stock market, Ely accepts a position as a clerk with the New York City Police Department.

AUGUST 14, 1878 · Birth of Maud Parker, Ely and Minnie's only child.

1881 · Ely meets Harriet Maxwell Converse, has extended correspondence with her, and advises her on her work with New York Indians and her writing.

AUGUST 30, 1895 · Death of Ely S. Parker. He is buried in Forest Lawn Cemetery on what was part of the Buffalo Creek Reservation, next to the grave of Red Jacket.

NOTES

1: A MEETING AT APPOMATTOX

3 "In my rough traveling suit": Ulysses S. Grant, *Personal Memoirs of Ulysses S. Grant* (New York: Charles L. Webster, 1886).

3 "The Staff had a little jollification of their own": Ely S. Parker, quoted in Sylvanus Cadwaller, *General Ely S. Parker's Narrative* (1893), 323.

4–8 All remaining quotes in chapter 1: *Arthur C. Parker, The Life of General Ely S. Parker* (Buffalo, NY: Buffalo Historical Society, 1919), 129–34.

2: WHO ARE THE IROQUOIS?

9 "The ancient League . . . strength": Ely S. Parker Papers, American Philosophical Society Library, letter dated July 22, 1887.

11 "We were the worst people in the world back then": Chief Jake Swamp, interviewed by Joseph Bruchac (unpublished), 1993.

20 "Brothers—The President is pleased with seeing you all in good health": Arthur C. Parker, *The Code of Handsome Lake, The Seneca Prophet, New York State Museum Bulletin* 163 (1913): 10.

23 "Move over . . . left to go": This is my own telling of a story I have heard from numerous Iroquois elders over the years and have been telling myself for over forty years. Another version of it can be found in *Red Jacket, Iroquois Diplomat and Orator* by Christopher Densmore. Syracuse, NY: Syracuse University Press, 1999, 91.

3: OF NOBLE BIRTH

27 "That the General . . . New York": Ely S. Parker, *Writings of General Parker*. Buffalo, NY: Buffalo Historical Society Publication, vol. 8, 1905, 520–36.

30   "Unite, my brethren!": Arthur C. Parker, *Red Jacket: Last of the Seneca* (New York: McGraw-Hill, 1952), 204–5.

4: THE RAINBOW DREAM

33   "That the mysterious . . . divine": Arthur C. Parker, *The Life of General Ely S. Parker*. Buffalo Historical Society, 1919 (reissue by Schroeder Publications, 2005).

35   "A son will be born to you": Arthur C. Parker, *The Life of General Ely S. Parker* (Buffalo, NY: Buffalo Historical Society, 1919), 48.

35   "I must . . . right here, disclaim any knowledge": Ibid., 174.

36   "I sometimes envy people with birthdays": Ibid., 172.

5: THE WHITE MAN'S SCHOOLS

39   "Beginning . . . book learning . . .": Parker, *Writings of General Parker*, 528.

40   "Now this is the way obtained by the Creator": Arthur C. Parker, *The Code of Handsome Lake, The Seneca Prophet, New York State Museum Bulletin* 163 (1913): 34.

41   "she had an ax . . . any man": Parker, *The Life of General Ely S. Parker*, 233.

42   "Now another message to tell your relatives": Ibid., 38.

43   "One of these mission stations": Ely S. Parker, *Writings of General Parker*, vol. 8 (Buffalo, NY: Buffalo Historical Society, 1905), 578.

44   "I understood very little of the English language": Ibid., 580.

45   "One Sunday, the missionary": Arthur C. Parker, *The Life of General Ely S. Parker* (Buffalo, NY: Buffalo Historical Society, 1919), 235.

46   "Here I made good and rapid progress": Parker, *Writings of General Parker*, 580.

47　"After one or two years": Ibid.

47　"the city of Hamilton . . . Lake Ontario": Parker, *Writings of General Parker*, 530.

48　"It was natural": Ibid.

48　"I bethought myself": Ibid.

50　"I have been engaged": Ely S. Parker, *Address at Yates Academy, April 18, 1843,* Ely S. Parker Papers, Buffalo and Erie County Historical Society, Buffalo, New York. Quoted in William H. Armstrong, *Warrior in Two Camps: Ely S. Parker, Union General and Seneca Chief* (Syracuse, NY: Syracuse University Press, 1978), 18.

51　"His was a noble": Letter by Mrs. Louise Bachelder, as quoted in Parker, *The Life of General Ely S. Parker*, 235.

51　"Although Parker possessed": Ibid.

6: A MEETING IN ALBANY

59　"To sound the war whoop and seize the youth": William H. Armstrong, *Warrior in Two Camps: Ely S. Parker, Union General and Seneca Chief* (Syracuse, NY: Syracuse University Press, 1978), 1.

60　"the great high priest . . ." and "a fine-looking man . . .": William H. Armstrong, *Warrior in Two Camps.* Syracuse, NY: Syracuse University Press, 1978, 3.

7: A HIGHER EDUCATION

62　"After remaining two years at this institution": Ely S. Parker, *Writings of General Parker, vol. 8 (Buffalo, NY:* Buffalo Historical Society, 1905), 580.

64　"I have generally been used well": William H. Armstrong, *Warrior in Two Camps: Ely S. Parker, Union General and Seneca Chief* (Syracuse, NY: Syracuse University Press, 1978), 22.

64 "The Indian . . . sees the Great Spirit": Ibid., 24.

65 "a close student and an apt scholar": Armstrong, *Warrior in Two Camps*, 24.

8: AN INDIAN IN WASHINGTON

68 "Oh, how I do long for": Ely S. Parker, *Diary Entry, February 9, 1846,* Ely S. Parker Papers, Buffalo and Erie County Historical Society, Buffalo, New York. Quoted in William H. Armstrong, *Warrior in Two Camps: Ely S. Parker, Union General and Seneca Chief* (Syracuse, NY: Syracuse University Press, 1978), 24.

69 "Hurra for Polk!": Ely S. Parker letter. Quoted in ibid., 25.

71 "as many as four pistols each": Armstrong, *Warrior in Two Camps*, 28.

72 "We have ever felt a strong friendship": Ely S. Parker, appeal to President Polk. Quoted in ibid., 28.

73 "There is no one . . . half so well": Armstrong, *Warrior in Two Camps*, 29.

73 "They look wild enough": Ely S. Parker, letter to Reuben Warren, June 25–26, 1846. Quoted in ibid., 30.

74 "Would you like a ride . . . thank you kindly" and "Some of our people here . . . great business": Armstrong, *Warrior in Two Camps*, 38.

77 "close inspection": Ely S. Parker, quoted in ibid., 32.

78 "tend to strongly unsettle . . . Indian policy": U.S. Congress, Senate Document No. 156, 29th Congress, 2nd Session, 1–2.

9: A LAWYER, AN ENGINEER

79 "They are represented": Ely S. Parker, quoted in William H. Armstrong, *Warrior in Two Camps: Ely S. Parker, Union General and Seneca Chief* (Syracuse, NY: Syracuse University Press, 1978), 33.

82 "all but to death . . . the Company": Letter of Ely S. Parker to Reuben Warren, November 11, 1847, Warren papers, State Historical Society of Wisconsin, Madison, Wisconsin.

83 "Go home . . . and wait" and "did then . . . Parker": Parker, *Writings of General Parker*, 525.

84 "attractive and genial": *Republican Advocate*, Batavia, N.Y., May 13, 1861.

10: THE LEAGUE OF THE HO-DE-NO-SAU-NEE

91 "Among the rarer relics": Arthur C. Parker, *The Life of General Ely S. Parker* (Buffalo, NY: Buffalo Historical Society, 1919), 89.

95 "It remains for the author": Lewis Henry Morgan, *League of the Iroquois* (New York: Corinth, 1962), xi.

95 "To encourage a kinder feeling": Ibid., ix.

96 "future elevation": *League of the Ho-de-no-sau-nee, Or Iroquois* by Lewis Henry Morgan, Rochester, 1851, 449.

100 "The thickness of your skin": from Arthur C. Parker, *The Constitution of the Five Nations, New York State Museum Bulletin* 158 (1911): 38.

100 "At my installation as leading Sachem": Ely S. Parker, letter to Geo. S. Conover, Esq., March 9, 1891. Quoted in Parker, *The Life of General Ely S. Parker*, 328.

11: A VICTORY AT LAST

104 "They do not want it": Ely S. Parker, "Notes on the Road," January 8–18, 1848, Ely S. Parker Papers, American Philosophical Society Library, Philadelphia, Pennsylvania.

105 "advance the cultural life" and "more compatible with our republican institutions": Armstrong, *Warrior in Two Camps*, 55.

106 "The Southern rebellion . . . Mexican war": *Personal Memoirs of General Ulysses S. Grant* (1885), Chapter 3.

106 "there is not an officer on my staff": Colonel Henry Fairchild, quoted in William H. Armstrong, *Warrior in Two Camps: Ely S. Parker, Union General and Seneca Chief* (Syracuse, NY: Syracuse University Press, 1978), 56.

110 "nearly ninety-nine . . . this region": Enclosures with Ely S. Parker and N.H. Parker to Franklin Pierce, October 17, 1856, Records of the Office of Indian Affairs, Letters Received, National Archives and Records Service, Washington, D.C. (records group 75).

112 "Notwithstanding the President's order": Ely S. Parker, quoted in ibid., 66.

12: A GENTLEMAN, THO' AN INDIAN

116 "a Civil Engineer of known and tried capacity": Ely S. Parker, quoted in William H. Armstrong, *Warrior in Two Camps: Ely S. Parker, Union General and Seneca Chief* (Syracuse, NY: Syracuse University Press, 1978), 61.

117 "the atrocious efforts of pot house politicians to remove Parker" and "a gentleman, tho' an Indian": Letters of Richard H. Jackson to

Howell Cobb, July 28 and August 30, 1857, National Archives and Records Service, Washington, D.C. (records group 121).

118-119 "the most perfect . . . of everyone": Armstrong, *Warrior in Two Camps*, 71.

13: TWO MILITARY MEN

120 "My acquaintance . . . he was": *Personal Recollections of the War of the Rebellion*, edited by James Grant Wilson and Titus Munson Coen, 1896, 344–45.

124 "Selling goods from behind a counter": Ely S. Parker, quoted in William H. Armstrong, *Warrior in Two Camps: Ely S. Parker, Union General and Seneca Chief* (Syracuse, NY: Syracuse University Press, 1978), 74.

124-125 "a warm and sympathetic nature . . . my Indian friends" and "saw him frequently . . . of his death": Wilson and Cohen, *Personal Recollections of the War of the Rebellion*, 344–45.

14: AN OFFER TO SERVE

128 "never suspected . . . systematically" and "I do not expect . . . position": Letter from Ely S. Parker to S.M. Clark, April 8, 1861, National Archives and Records Service (records group 121).

129 "Do you know": Ely S. Parker, quoted in William H. Armstrong, *Warrior in Two Camps: Ely S. Parker, Union General and Seneca Chief* (Syracuse, NY: Syracuse University Press, 1978), 79.

131 "Go home": Ely S. Parker, quoted in Arthur C. Parker, *The Life of General Ely S. Parker* (Buffalo, NY: Buffalo Historical Society, 1919), 103.

132 "is a freeholder": Ely S. Parker, quoted in Armstrong, *Warrior in Two Camps,* 78.

132 "while my hands labor . . . other scenes" and "This sad and awful bereavement . . . our family": Ely S. Parker to N.H. Parker, February 23, 1862, Ely S, Parker papers, American Philosophical Society Library.

15: AS MUCH UNDER FIRE

135 "I was at Vicksburg . . . again": Parker, *Writings of General Parker,* 525.

136 "a good practical Civil Engineer" and "bore the seal . . . War Department" and "white man's war": Parker, *The Life of General Ely S. Parker,* 166.

137 "Who will be our friend . . ." and "I am determined . . . all right": Parker, *The Life of General Ely S. Parker,* 166.

137 "My commanding general and myself": Ely S. Parker, quoted in William H. Armstrong, *Warrior in Two Camps: Ely S. Parker, Union General and Seneca Chief* (Syracuse, NY: Syracuse University Press, 1978), 86.

138 "a hard-looking . . . himself" and "one vast cemetery . . . of the ground": Letter from Ely S. Parker to H. J. Ensign, July 29, 1863 in the *Republican Advocate,* August 18, 1863.

138 "My horse stepped on": Ibid.

139 "a mosaic . . . family friends": Armstrong, *Warrior in Two Camps,* 87.

141 "after a severe illness": Ely S. Parker, quoted in Arthur C. Parker, *The Life of General Ely S. Parker* (Buffalo, NY: Buffalo Historical Society, 1919), 110.

NOTES

142 "It has been a matter of universal": Ely S. Parker, quoted in Armstrong, *Warrior in Two Camps, Ely S. Parker,* 90.

143 "You dislodged him": Grant's order, quoted in ibid., 91.

145 "never disturbed . . . events" and "his silent desk . . . moment" and "now afloat . . . wide world": Letter from Ely S. Parker to J. E. Smith, Bender Collection, Wyoming State Archives and History Department.

16: WE ARE ALL AMERICANS

150 "Grant never cared much": Ely S. Parker, quoted in William H. Armstrong, *Warrior in Two Camps: Ely S. Parker, Union General and Seneca Chief* (Syracuse, NY: Syracuse University Press, 1978), 91.

151 "I developed . . . rebel lines": Parker, *The Life of General Ely S. Parker,* 111.

152 "Parker, do you know . . . after me": Parker, *The Life of General Ely S. Parker,* 112.

152 "After the battle I met": Ely S. Parker, quoted in Arthur C. Parker, *The Life of General Ely S. Parker* (Buffalo, NY: Buffalo Historical Society, 1919), 11–112.

153 "We shall not leave this house": Ibid., 114.

154 "outlined his plans . . . would requite": Parker, *The Life of General Ely S. Parker,* 120.

155 Letter: Parker, *The Life of General Ely S. Parker,* 121.

156 Letter: Parker, *The Life of General Ely S. Parker,* 126.

157 "That apple tree . . . on my watch-chain": Parker, *Writings of General Parker,* 534–35.

158 "spoke feelingly . . . represented": Armstrong, *Warrior in Two Camps,* 111.

159 "Grant's favored aid . . . dusky-faced" and "You white men . . . a friend": *Rochester Union and Advertiser*, May 26, 1865.

17: INDIAN AFFAIRS

163 "very well pleased . . . west": Letter from Ely S. Parker to Nic Parker, October 27, 1865, Harry E. Huntington Library, San Marino, CA.

163 "an absolute necessity" and "unreconstructed": Ely S. Parker's report of January 27, 1866, included in a letter from E. M. Stanton to the president, February 15, 1866, A. Johnson Papers, Library of Congress.

164 "To guard against an unjust oppression": Ely S. Parker, quoted in William H. Armstrong, *Warrior in Two Camps: Ely S. Parker, Union General and Seneca Chief* (Syracuse, NY: Syracuse University Press, 1978), 117.

164 "Hardly any thing . . . the matter" and "a permanent and perpetual peace . . . tribes": Armstrong, *Warrior in Two Camps*, 119.

164 First, Indian Affairs: Ibid., 119–20.

166 "adopt the habits . . . communities": U.S. Congress, House Misc. Document No. 37, 39th Congress, 2nd Session.

169 The wedding was planned: Parker, *The Life of General Ely S. Parker*, 145–46.

171 "Some people thought I married": Ely S. Parker, quoted in Armstrong, *Warrior in Two Camps*, 132.

18: THE INDIAN COMMISSIONER

172 "The Indian . . . Office": Annual Report of the Commission of Indian Affairs (1869), page 484, Records of the Office of Indian

Affairs, Report Books, 19:98, National Archives and Records Service (records group 75).

173 "think of no one . . . country": Letter from John M. Thayer to President Ulysses S. Grant, March 6, 1869, National Archives and Records Service (records group 48).

173 "habits, in the manner of drinking": Letter from Asher Wright to S. B. Treat, April 9, 1869, National Archives and Records Service (records group 48).

173 "appointment will . . . to the Indian": Ibid.

174 "Grant could not do better": Asher Wright, quoted in William H. Armstrong, *Warrior in Two Camps: Ely S. Parker, Union General and Seneca Chief* (Syracuse, NY: Syracuse University Press, 1978), 135.

175 "When he . . . away his things": Charles Lewis Slattery, Felix Reville Brunot. Longmans (1901), 145.

177 "the inevitable change of their mode": Ely S. Parker, quoted in ibid., 141.

177 "eminent for their . . . philanthropy": Armstrong, *Warrior in Two Camps*, 143.

178 "the religion . . . any people": Annual Report of the Board of Indian Commissioners (1869), 492.

180 "more than suspected fraud": Letter from Jacob Cox to William Welsh, July 5, 1869, Cox Papers, Oberlin College Archives.

180 "Hasn't the old man come yet?": Armstrong, *Warrior in Two Camps*, 145.

181 "General Parker . . . wife": Armstrong, *Warrior in Two Camps*, 145.

181 "His wife is fair": *New York Herald* article, quoted in ibid., 146.

182 "Our holy religion . . . heathen people": Armstrong, *Warrior in Two Camps*, 152.

182 "a full report of his past life to date," "covering their tracks," and "Colonel Parker . . . ring": Letter from E.P. Smith to George Whipple, December 15, 1870, American Missionary Association Archives, Amistad Research Center, Dillard University, New Orleans, LA.

183 "Although the consequences were deplorable": Ely S. Parker, quoted in ibid., 147.

184 "poor and naked": Annual Report of the Board of Indian Commissioners (1870), 38.

185 "Here is the Commissioner of Indian Affairs": Quoted in ibid., 149.

186 "like the handle . . . one side": Parker, *Writings of General Parker*, 532.

187 "now has power . . . obey him": Armstrong, *Warrior in Two Camps*, 149.

187 "It was only . . . agencies": Armstrong, *Warrior in Two Camps*, 149.

187 "We must feed . . . Indians": Armstrong, *Warrior in Two Camps*, 150.

190 "irregularities, neglect, and incompetence": U.S. Congress, House Report No. 39, 41st Congress, 3rd Session, 3233.

190 "We have no evidence": Quoted in ibid., 159.

190 "Your resignation": Ulysses S. Grant, quoted in ibid., 160.

19: I AM A MAN

191 "Why should . . . the gallon?": Parker, *The Life of General Ely S. Parker*, 9.

192 "one of the reigning belles of Washington": Armstrong, *Warrior in Two Camps*, 162.

195 "a widely read man": George Mills, quoted in William H. Armstrong, *Warrior in Two Camps: Ely S. Parker, Union General and Seneca Chief* (Syracuse, NY: Syracuse University Press, 1978), 164.

NOTES

196 "General Parker's lawyers": Arthur C. Parker, *The Life of General Ely S. Parker* (Buffalo, NY: Buffalo Historical Society, 1919), 160.

197 "While I was soldiering . . . the places": Parker, *Writings of General Parker*, 535.

200 "loosen up my tongue": Parker, *The Life of General Ely S. Parker*, 117.

201 "I'm a real American and the only one here." Armstrong, *Warrior in Two Camps*, 189.

201 "the perfect diarrhea . . . controversies": Letter from Ely S. Parker to J. E. Smith, March 15, 1886 (HM EG, Box 45), Henry E. Huntington Library, San Marino, CA.

202 "I loved your father . . . sincerely": Ibid.

202 "There are a great many things that I could say": Ely S. Parker, quoted in Armstrong, *Warrior in Two Camps*, 173.

208 "When they abandon their birth right": Parker, *The Life of General Ely S. Parker*, 176.

210 "I am an aged tree and can stand no longer . . .": Parker, *The Life of General Ely S. Parker*, 212.

211 "Some impish impulse": Ely S. Parker, quoted in Armstrong, *Warrior in Two Camps*, 189.

212 "The General," she wrote: Armstrong, *Warrior in Two Camps*, 191.

217 "We are much gratified": Parker, *The Life of General Ely S. Parker*, 226.

BIBLIOGRAPHY

Armstrong, William H. *Warrior in Two Camps: Ely S. Parker, Union General and Seneca Chief.* Syracuse, NY: Syracuse University Press, 1978.

Bolton, Jonathan and Claire Wilson. *Joseph Brant: Mohawk Chief.* Broomall, PA: Chelsea House, 1992.

Hauptman, Lawrence M. *The Iroquois in the Civil War: From Battlefield to Reservation.* Syracuse, NY: Syracuse University Press, 1993.

———— *The Tonawanda Senecas' Heroic Battle Against Removal.* Syracuse, NY: Syracuse University Press, 2011.

Morgan, Lewis Henry. *League of the Ho-de-no-sau-nee, or Iroquois.* Rochester, NY: Sage and Brothers, 1851.

Parker, Arthur C. *The Life of General Ely S. Parker: Last Grand Sachem of the Iroquois and General Grant's Military* Secretary. Buffalo, NY: Buffalo Historical Society, 1919.

————. *Red Jacket: Last of the Seneca.* New York: McGraw-Hill, 1952.

IMAGE CREDITS

All image captions include dates, when available.

ACKNOWLEDGMENTS

I first became fascinated with the story of Ely Parker fifty years ago while visiting the Six Nations Museum in Onchiota, New York. The museum's founder, Ray Tehanetorens Fadden, introduced me to Ely's extraordinary life. In the decades that followed I found myself learning more through the books written by Parker's grand-nephew Arthur C. Parker. He was one of Ray's friends, and his medicine pouch still hangs high from a buffalo head in that museum now run by Ray's grandson. My understanding of Ely Parker also has deepened through my access to his own extensive writing—thanks in particular to the wonderful work of the Buffalo History Museum.

Just as important in understanding his life and the resilient native nation which he represented as a "Grand Sachem" has been my contacts over the years with such Seneca friends, storytellers, and historians as Michele "Midge" Dean Stock, Peter Jemison, Darwin Hill, Duce Bowen, and John Mohawk.

I also need to gratefully acknowledge the work done by Lawrence Hauptman and William H. Armstrong. Hauptman's books on the Tonawanda Senecas and Native Americans in the Civil War are deeply informative and insightful. Armstrong's *Warrior in Two Camps* is still the best book written about Parker. Special thanks to Doug Kanentiio George (Akwesasne Mohawk) for his close reading of the manuscript and his helpful suggestions.

INDEX

Note: Page numbers in *italics* refer to illustrations.

INDEX